Editor-in-Chief and Founder:
  Lyndon H. LaRouche, Jr.
Editorial Board: *Lyndon H. LaRouche, Jr. , Helga
  Zepp-LaRouche, Robert Ingraham, Tony
  Papert, Gerald Rose, Dennis Small, Jeffrey
  Steinberg, William Wertz*
Co-Editors: *Robert Ingraham, Tony Papert*
Managing Editor: *Nancy Spannaus*
Technology: *Marsha Freeman*
Books: *Katherine Notley*
Ebooks: *Richard Burden*
Graphics: *Alan Yue*
Photos: *Stuart Lewis*
Circulation Manager: *Stanley Ezrol*

INTELLIGENCE DIRECTORS
Counterintelligence: *Jeffrey Steinberg, Michele
  Steinberg*
Economics: *John Hoefle, Marcia Merry Baker,
  Paul Gallagher*
History: *Anton Chaitkin*
Ibero-America: *Dennis Small*
Russia and Eastern Europe: *Rachel Douglas*
United States: *Debra Freeman*

INTERNATIONAL BUREAUS
Bogotá: *Miriam Redondo*
Berlin: *Rainer Apel*
Copenhagen: *Tom Gillesberg*
Houston: *Harley Schlanger*
Lima: *Sara Madueño*
Melbourne: *Robert Barwick*
Mexico City: *Gerardo Castilleja Chávez*
New Delhi: *Ramtanu Maitra*
Paris: *Christine Bierre*
Stockholm: *Ulf Sandmark*
United Nations, N.Y.C.: *Leni Rubinstein*
Washington, D.C.: *William Jones*
Wiesbaden: *Göran Haglund*

ON THE WEB
e-mail: eirns@larouchepub.com
www.larouchepub.com
www.executiveintelligencereview.com
www.larouchepub.com/eiw
Webmaster: *John Sigerson*
Assistant Webmaster: *George Hollis*
Editor, Arabic-language edition: *Hussein Askary*

EIR (ISSN 0273-6314) *is published weekly
(50 issues), by EIR News Service, Inc.,
P.O. Box 17390, Washington, D.C. 20041-0390.
(703) 297-8434*

European Headquarters: E.I.R. GmbH, Postfach
Bahnstrasse 9a, D-65205, Wiesbaden, Germany
Tel: 49-611-73650
Homepage: http://www.eir.de
e-mail: info@eir.de
Director: Georg Neudecker

Montreal, Canada: 514-461-1557
eir@eircanada.ca

Denmark: EIR - Danmark, Sankt Knuds Vej 11,
basement left, DK-1903 Frederiksberg, Denmark.
Tel.: +45 35 43 60 40, Fax: +45 35 43 87 57. e-mail:
eirdk@hotmail.com.

Mexico City: EIR, Sor Juana Inés de la Cruz 242-2
Col. Agricultura C.P. 11360
Delegación M. Hidalgo, México D.F.
Tel. (5525) 5318-2301
eirmexico@gmail.com

Postmaster: Send all address changes to *EIR*, P.O.
Box 17390, Washington, D.C. 20041-0390.

Signed articles in *EIR* represent the views of the authors,
and not necessarily those of the Editorial Board.

The Dawn of A New Era

EIR Contents

www.larouchepub.com Volume 44, Number 21, May 26, 2017

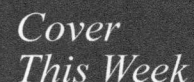

Ocean's Bridge, 1862, by American artist Martin Johnson Heade.

I. The New System and Its Opponents

New Silk Road Goes Global, Including in the U.S.—This Is the Reason Trump is Under Attack

by Michael Billington

May 17—As world leaders returned to their home countries from the historic Belt and Road Forum for International Cooperation which took place in Beijing on May 14-15, they are proudly announcing to their citizens and to the world that a new paradigm for world affairs has been established, both economically and culturally. In a very real sense, the title of the *EIR* Special Report from 2014—*The New Silk Road Becomes the World Land-Bridge*—is becoming a reality.)

Look around the world:

Europe

Italian Prime Minister Paolo Gentiloni, after attending the Beijing forum and later meeting with Russian President Vladimir Putin in Sochi, described the Belt and Road Forum as "an event that could leave a trail in history in the next years, because it is a project tending to be a global project." He said that "launching this bridge between Asia and Europe also has a political significance, besides the physical, economic one. Italy has decided to join at a high level— the only G7 country to do so—to give a signal of sharing." (Actually, both Japan and the United States also took dramatic steps towards full engagement in the Belt and Road—see below)

One example in Italy: The Italians are expanding, with Chinese help, the North Adriatic Port Association (NAPA) which includes the ports of Venice in Italy, Trieste and Kober in Slovenia, and Rijeka in Croatia. The expansion will upgrade existing ports and build a new port off-shore from Venice which will be able to handle container ships. New rail lines into northern Europe will make the upper Adriatic another hub for the rapidly expanding trade between Europe and Asia.

Zivadin Jovanovic of Serbia, who heads the Belgrade Forum for a World of Equals, wrote on May 15: "Once again China has demonstrated the vision and magnetism of the new pattern of 'win-win' cooperation for the new era of the multipolar world. The pattern radiates equality, openness, and mutual benefit, not pro-

Heads of State and Heads of Government who participated in the Belt and Road Forum for International Cooperation in Beijing on May 14-15.

kremlin.ru

China is partnering in the upgrading of the port of Trieste to develop North Adriatic ports as the western terminal of the Maritime Silk Road.

tectionism and power politics." He reports that the Chinese are building a rail connection linking Serbia with the South Adriatic along the eastern shore of the Adriatic to Greece. In addition, the construction of the Belgrade-Budapest High-Speed Railway, which has been stalled by EU interference, will start in November. "It will be the biggest construction undertaking in the whole of Europe," he writes.

Greek Prime Minister Alexis Tsipras

Greek Prime Minister Alexis Tsipras, who attended the Beijing Forum, spoke of the original Silk Road: "If we were to retell, today, the history of the Silk Road, we would not only retell an economic history of cooperation and competition between great powers, religions, nations, and commercial interests, but a history of people, their contact and communication. The commercial and cultural contacts of the Greek and Chinese people stretch back thousands of years. They have traded, worked with each other, travelled to each others lands, and inspired each other with their struggles."

On the New Silk Road, he added: "This Initiative is based on the development of Infrastructure and Connectivity projects bringing Europe and Asia, as well as other parts of the world, closer together. But if it remains only a series of projects, it will not fulfill the vision on which it is based. It will not be a vibrant Silk Road of the 21st Century. The Belt and Road Initiative gives us a remarkable platform with which to connect initiatives enhancing people-to-people contact, and I believe we should make full use of it." Tsipras had hosted the "First Forum of Ancient Civilizations" in Athens in April, cosponsored by Greece and China, the cradles of western and eastern civilization, respectively.

Czech President Milos Zeman

Czech President Milos Zeman mocked those who complain that the Belt and Road is dividing Europe, saying that Europe is already horribly divided, but can be united through the common mission of the Silk Road.

Prime Minister of Hungary Viktor Orban

Hungary's Prime Minister Viktor Orban told his nation that many countries were sick of lectures on human rights and free markets (such as those from the European Union), and that the "old model of globalization is dead," as the Silk Road is creating a development-based global paradigm.

Asia

Japan's high-level representative to the forum in Beijing was Toshihiro Nikai, the head of the ruling Liberal Democratic Party. Nikai met personally with Chinese President Xi Jinping, to discuss the potential for Japan to join the Asian Infrastructure Investment Bank (AIIB) initiated by China, and to plan an exchange of visits between President Xi and Japanese Prime Minister Shinzo Abe. Abe indicated that he would carefully discuss these matters with President Trump, who had indicated that it was a mistake for the United States (under Obama) to boycott the AIIB. Abe had been under intense pressure from Obama not to join the bank. It is possible that Abe and Trump are considering joining the AIIB at the same time.

Philippine President Duterte announced upon his return from the forum that there are plans to restore the 2005 program for joint development of the rich resources of the South China Sea with China and Vietnam, now that Obama's plan for war in the South China Sea has been rejected all across Asia. The 2005 program was sabotaged by anti-China forces within the Philippines. President Trump has moved to restore close cooperation with both China and the Philippines.

Philippines Presidential website
Philippine President
Rodrigo Duterte

Ibero America

The nations of South and Central America had been less directly involved in the early stages of the Silk Road process, but following the Beijing forum, many are saying that the Americas are now fully on board. The head of the U.N. Economic Commission for Latin America and the Caribbean, Alicia Barcena, who attended the forum, praised the Belt and Road Initiative as "a renewal of the profound commitment to the values that are fundamental for our global economic and social well-being," and called on all the member nations to "harness the potential that this One Belt One Road has for redefining capitalism through people's equality and dignity."

The head of the Inter-American Development Bank, Luis Alberto Moreno, declared that Latin America is now very much part of the Silk Road initiative, which is "not only a limited group of countries, but the entire world."

youtube
IADB President
Luis Alberto Moreno

Africa

Kenyan President Uhuru Kenyatta said upon his return, "The Belt and Road Initiative gives our continent the opportunity to make a paradigm-shift. Post-colonial Africa has been stuck in a rut. Being part of One Belt allows the continent to move to a new platform, through which global collaboration will allow for value-addition, innovation, and increased prosperity." Note that the notion of a "new paradigm" and lifting the global "platform" of productivity have been the core concepts of the LaRouche movement's historic campaign for the New Silk Road and the World Land-Bridge.

wikipedia
Kenyan President
Uhuru Kenyatta

Similar enthusiastic responses fill the press of nations across the developing sector.

United States

And in the United States? Virtually unknown to the American population, the Trump Administration representative to the Beijing Forum, Matthew Pottinger, set up an "American Belt and Road Working Group," to bring American companies into the Silk Road process! Beyond that, he invited China to attend the "SelectUSA Investment Summit," on June 18-20 in Washington, D.C., to include China in investment opportunities in the United States.

youtube/KBS news
Matthew Pottinger

On May 17, Tu Guangshao, president of the China Investment Corporation (CIC) sovereign wealth fund, told the *Wall Street Journal,* "there is a potential for Chinese companies to make more investments in the United States and vice versa." Underscoring the Chinese initiative, on May 18 CIC is opening an office in New York City, replacing the one in Toronto, which until now had been CIC's only overseas representative office. Tu explained that CIC is particularly looking at U.S. projects in highways, rail, and high-tech manufacturing plants, emphasizing that CIC can become a stable source of long-term capital for United States infrastructure and manufacturing projects, as well as helping U.S. companies to expand their operations in China's market.

In January of this year, CIC chairman Ding Xuedong indicated that CIC wanted to change $50 billion of its holdings of United States Treasury debt into an investment in building of new infrastructure in the United States. Ding's estimate of the investment needed to build a new and modern economic infrastructure in America was $8 trillion—far beyond President Trump's $1 trillion program—which, he said, would not be invested by the U.S. government and private investors alone. Schiller Institute chairwoman Helga Zepp-LaRouche has enthusiastically supported such a proposal, noting that it would represent an exciting new level of Sino-U.S. collaboration to rebuild America's decaying infrastructure.

In his *Wall Street Journal* interview, Tu noted that, in the past, the U.S. government and Congress have frustrated CIC direct investment, and pointed to the "overly strict scrutiny and opaque investment-review process" of U.S. authorities during the Bush and Obama years. Major investments in ports, rail, and other infrastructure were rejected on "security" grounds. Perhaps now, under Trump, the United States will be open to the contribution China can make to reversing the nation's economic decay. (see the LaRouche PAC pamphlet, "America's Future on the New Silk Road").

Press Blackout

Any U.S. citizen dependent on the U.S. media or reports from the U.S. Congress, would know none of this. Rather, nearly the entirety of the 24-hour news cycle in the United States is composed of hysterical rants against President Trump. If any of it were to be believed, one would think the President is a puppet of evil Russia and evil China, who are out to take over the world and undermine the pristine values of Western Civilization, and that Trump is guilty of treason for doing what he promised to do in his campaign—ending the Bush and Obama "regime change" war policies, and restoring America's industry and infrastructure, and the jobs that go with it.

Do not believe the lie that Trump is on the defensive—that his actions have undermined his credibility, as peddled *ad nauseam* in the western media. The fact is, Trump is on the offensive, to end the British Imperial

cc/Northern Ireland Executive

Tu Guanshao (right), president of the China Investment Corporation (CIC) sovereign wealth fund, discussing investment and infrastructure opportunities with Northern Ireland Infrastructure Minister Chris Hazzard, on Oct 12, 2016 in Beijing.

era of history. The British and their assets in the United States—the neocons in both parties and on Wall Street, and the corrupt elements in the intelligence community, especially the FBI—are absolutely hysterical now that the geopolitical division of the world into warring factions, is being replaced with a win-win policy based on the common aims of mankind. What is at stake for this imperial oligarchy is their ability to induce the U.S. population to passively accept austerity and war, which is being destroyed by Trump's move to bring the United States into the New Silk Road, and to work with Russia to crush the terrorist scourge. His stated intention to restore Glass Steagall and the Hamiltonian American System of physical economy, simply drives the British assets further into panic mode.

As Helga Zepp-LaRouche reiterated in her many speeches and interviews in China this past weekend—she was a featured speaker at the Global Think Tank Summit at the Belt and Road Forum: if Donald Trump succeeds in bringing the United States into the new paradigm of the global Silk Road, he will be remembered as one of the great presidents of American history. The Belt and Road International Forum, she said, has set the world on a course to a final demise of Empire and the zero-sum game geopolitical mind-set that goes with it. This week there has been a dramatic phase shift in the history of humanity.

Paraphrasing Benjamin Franklin: There is now a new world economic order, if we can keep it.

Space Cooperation Is the Next Phase Of Development in Mankind's Future

by Kesha Rogers

Let both sides seek to invoke the wonders of science instead of its terrors. Together let us explore the stars, conquer the deserts, eradicate disease, tap the ocean depths and encourage the arts and commerce.

—President John F. Kennedy

May 23—Monday, May 29, will mark the 100th birthday anniversary of President John F. Kennedy. It is now both fitting—and a matter of great urgency—that we take this opportunity to reflect on President Kennedy and on his vision for the development of this nation. These reflections must take into account his tangible contributions to the development of peace around the planet, not just as some symbolic event, but to provide a fuller understanding of the quality of leadership that is needed today.

The determined vision expressed in President Kennedy's first inaugural address was one that shaped and drove his short presidency, before he was assassinated by the very same destructive forces who were determined not to allow such vision, or anything like it, to succeed.

President John F. Kennedy calling for the establishment of a Space Program at a Joint Session of Congress, May 25, 1961.

NASA

Lyndon LaRouche, as a leading physical economist, understood precisely the nature of the standard of economics that Kennedy drew upon. It is one that is absolutely opposed to a system of wealth defined by money. Kennedy, like Franklin Roosevelt and Lincoln before him, were defenders of the Hamiltonian System of Public Credit. This is the system that Lyndon LaRouche has continued to develop and advance throughout his life-long work. LaRouche has repeatedly pointed to the core principles of Alexander Hamilton's outlook as what is required today to replace the Wall Street free trade system that is now crumbling.

It is the prerogative of mankind to explore and to create new forms of technology, to explore the Solar system, to take dominion over the Solar system, and to advance the noëtic process of mankind. What does this mean in practice? It is not through the mere printing of money that we will increase productivity in our society, but by creating new discoveries, making new scientific breakthroughs, and increasing the standard of living and productive potential of every human being.

This requires not just the rebuilding of existing infrastructure. What we must insist upon today is a restored national mission, one which aims to increase the progress and cooperation among nations, through growth and physical-economic development.

At the recent Belt and Road Forum in Beijing—which was a true expression of win-win cooperation offered by China—Helga Zepp-LaRouche developed the required next phase of global cooperation in a speech she delivered to the concurrent think tank summit. She stressed the need for elevating mankind to the next level of cooperation. She asked,

Where do we want humanity and the world to be in ten, one hundred, or even one thousand years? Is it not the natural destiny of mankind, as the only creative species known in the universe, so far, that we will be building villages on the moon, developing a deeper understanding of trillions of galaxies in our universe, solving the problems of till now incurable diseases, or solving the problem of energy and raw materials security through the development of thermonuclear fusion power?

The Space Silk Road

The next phase of cooperation that the United States and China must immediately rise to, together with many other nations, requires the United States to join with the initiative of the Belt and Road, and from that initial step to move forward to worldwide cooperation in space exploration. We must advance the concept of a *Space Silk Road*, as China is already taking certain initiatives to do. We need to operate from the standpoint of looking at the next fifty years of mankind in the Solar System. What would a Space Silk Road entail? What do you envision that that would mean for the progress of mankind? How do you actually envision the conception of a Space Silk Road as a development and continuation of what has been developed and set forth in terms of the Maritime Silk Road and the trade routes, and the cooperation that has already been brought into being by the Belt and Road Initiative?

It is important, first, to understand that you are talking about the creation of new technologies, new scientific platforms that do not yet exist. When you're discussing the heritage of the historic Silk Road, one of the things that it was really known for—and you can read about the different transformations of ideas in astronomy, in mathematics—was the transformation and sharing of technology, the sharing of different resources, of foods, of supplies, between Europe and Asia. As travelers traversed these routes, you saw a sharing of inventions and scientific breakthroughs, in addition to the trade in silk, tea, rice, other goods, and cultural goods.

What we are discussing, and what now has to be the approach, is that we need to look at this idea of advancing the Silk Road into space, not just as sharing already existing technology, but first of all, the idea that you're taking the creative powers, the noëtic powers of the human mind, and expanding them out into the Solar system to make new discoveries; to make breakthroughs in the development of other planetary bodies, breakthroughs that are going to allow us to advance our understanding of how to increase the productivity of man here on Earth. That approach was already set forth and embedded in the policy of the United States space program originally set forth under President John F. Kennedy.

When Kennedy declaimed his vision for the space program in the 1960s, to land a man on the Moon and return him safely to Earth before the end of the decade, it was not some short-term gratification. We were talking about the process of creating new sciences, new technologies, that were going to advance mankind as a whole.

In Kennedy's famous speech on May 25, 1961, he laid out his vision before a Joint Session of Congress. That vision did not stop at something very small and superficial; it really developed the concept of the next phase of mankind. You have to think about this, about why this vision was enunciated at that time. First, Kennedy called for landing a man on the Moon and returning him safely to Earth. Many people stopped at that, but he didn't stop there: Second, he called for an additional $23 million, together with $7 million that was already available, to accelerate the development of the Rover nuclear rocket. He said:

> This gives promise of someday providing a means to even more exciting and ambitious exploration of space, perhaps beyond the Moon, perhaps to the very end of the Solar system itself.

In that speech, he then goes on to call for an additional $50 million, which "will make the most of our present leadership by accelerating the use of space satellites for worldwide communication." And finally, he calls for $75 million, of which $53 million was to go to the Weather Bureau, to give us a deeper understanding of the development of satellite systems.

It was never President John F. Kennedy's intention that a true exploration of space would be grounded in the realm of monetary profit, nor that it was a publicity stunt of sending someone on a one-way trip to Mars or getting to the Moon and planting a flag and saying, "Been there, done that." The idea, as Lyndon LaRouche has emphasized, has to start with the conception of creating new platforms of creative scientific development for the advancement of mankind, to advance and grow the productive power of the population.

This is now what you're seeing unfold, in what would constitute a *Belt and Road Space Initiative* for today. Obviously, you're going to have opposition. The intention of the British agents on Wall Street is to insist on their hereditary right to enforce a Malthusian policy, one which flows from their publicly stated view that there are too many people on the planet. They say: You should not allow nations to advance and have access to new forms of technology; you should definitely not—as they believe—give nations the opportunity to have access to fusion technology. So, they attack the development of fusion power; they attack the reality that we should have already been on the Moon with villages and colonies there, advancing the use of resources such as helium-3.

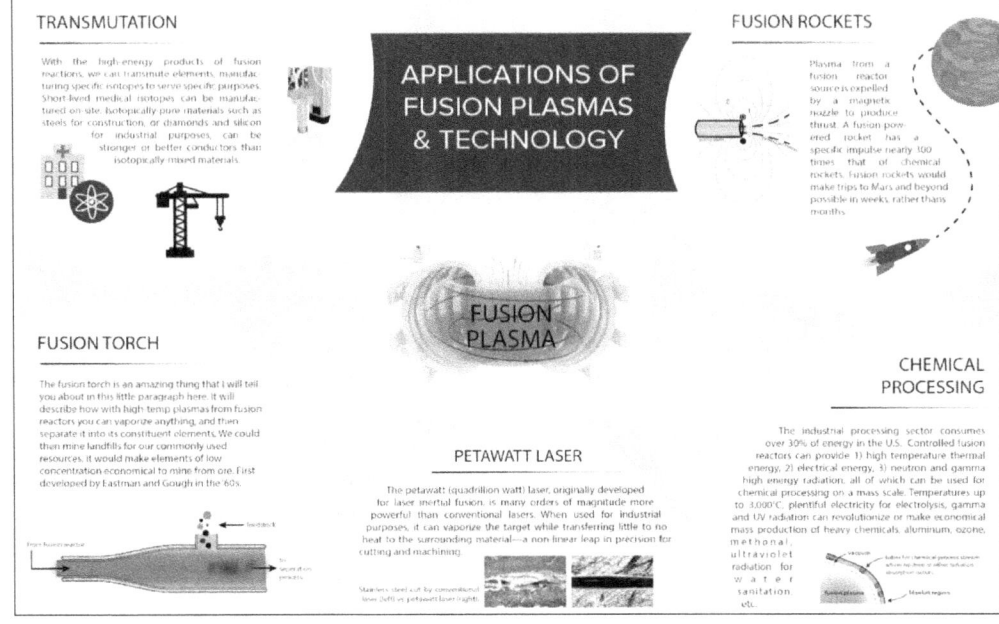

This potential future—these advances, which should have already been realized and were the initiatives that President Kennedy continued—is a future that Lyndon LaRouche proposed in his beautiful vision, a speech calling for the fulfillment of what Kennedy had begun, titled "The Woman on Mars."

The growth and development of mankind is the most important weapon for defeating the Empire, the enemy of mankind. Lyndon LaRouche's Moon-Mars colonization program called for a new economic platform and the rapid development of space technologies.

The Peaceful Progress of Mankind

China's offer of "win-win cooperation" is really a continuation of the decades-long fight of Lyndon and Helga LaRouche. That principled fight expresses something that goes way beyond just basic praise and agreement among nations. It goes to the heart of dedicating ourselves to the peaceful progress of mankind for the benefit of all. That outlook has been captured in the mission and vision set forth in China's space program, which is taking the lead right now, because China is not dedicating its space program to private-sector commercial space flights that only seek to make profit. Rather, they are thinking about nations working together for the benefit of the whole. This is precisely what they have enunciated. In an official white paper, issued just at the end of last year, the vision China lays out is very much in line with the national mission that was set forth by President John F. Kennedy, the mission to which Mr. LaRouche has dedicated his life.

The Chinese make the point that their intention is to explore outer space and to enhance our understanding of the Earth and the cosmos; to utilize outer space for peaceful purposes and promote human civilizations and social progress for the benefit of the whole of mankind; to meet the demands of economic, scientific, and technological development, national security, and social progress; and to improve the scientific and cultural levels of the Chinese people.

Now, I have to say, China recognizes—just as President John F. Kennedy recognized when he made the offer of cooperation to the Soviet Union in 1963 for a joint mission on the Moon—that this development of outer space is not going to be done by one nation or one group of people, but by all people and by all nations. Coming out of the Belt and Road Forum, the peaceful progress and development of space, in partnership with other nations, is our natural orientation.

Today, by joining in the Belt and Road Initiative, we are poised to join such an endeavor. This poses the immediate challenge of rising to the next level of the progress of mankind, the development of fusion power, putting the development of fusion technology back on the table immediately and reversing the trend of thirty, forty-plus years of physical-economic sabotage. In contrast to the mind of President Kennedy, our last President openly derided the need for the advancements of new scientific platforms, stating publicly, "We don't need any fancy fusion"—the same President who shut down our space program and actually turned it over to the monetary hitmen.

We have to reverse that! The Belt and Road Initiative has now given us a gateway to move mankind forward with this potential for international cooperation in space exploration, as is absolutely necessary to free mankind from the British imperial system of neocolonialism, usury, and human degradation—to bring about the advance of man in the formation of new scientific platforms, new technologies, and new human discoveries.

DR. AHMED AL-KEDIDI

Hope for the Future: The New Silk Road

This article was published in Arabic in several Gulf newspapers on May 22, as President Trump visited the region to meet heads of state of Arab and Muslim nations. It has been translated and edited by EIR. *The author, Dr. Ahmed Al-Kedidi, is a former Tunisian diplomat and former advisor to the Emir of Qatar, and is now resident in Doha, Qatar.*

May 21—Certain important events this week brought joy to me personally, because they confirmed for me that I was right in taking the decision, three decades ago, to join in the project to change the evils of the unjust trans-Atlantic world order, and replace it with a new and just world order established on the foundations of cooperation and inclusion of all nations in development, and achieving lasting peace on the basis of connecting nations and continents through railway networks, bridges, and tunnels, and facilitating the movement of people, goods, and ideas on land, sea, and air.

What is odd in our recent history in Tunisia, is that when my friend Mohammad Mazali became Prime Minister in 1980, he worked in this correct direction, and we were all committed to follow his sound path.

He established the education system on the method of Arabization. He then opened the door of south-south cooperation, and we reached agreements with China and Turkey. We opened banks and corporations in cooperation with the Gulf countries, and enhanced exchange and integration among Tunisia, Algeria, and Morocco—which was politically and culturally diametrically opposite to the methods of President Habib Bourgiba, whose policies were solely based on the con-

Schiller Institute

Dr. Ahmed Al-Kedidi

nection with France as a doctrine of dependency, not national interest.

For our efforts, we were persecuted by those who benefitted from putting Tunisia under the arm of France. We endured the witch-hunt of Interpol with patience, and had to suffer fifteen years of exile, our families separated, and our homes confiscated.

The cultural option we joined, traces its origins from the Silk Road, which was under the patronage of China many centuries ago, and which constituted a belt of economic, commercial, and cultural exchange among nations.

One of the new events which has brought renewed hope to my soul, is the participation of my honorable friend, Mrs. Helga Zepp-LaRouche, founder and chairman of the international Schiller Institutes, in the Beijing Forum for International Development last week at the invitation of the President of China, Xi Jinping. The Forum focussed on the theme of reactivating the Silk Road, and had the participation of many statesmen from different continents, to launch a new era, an era not controlled by the powerful trans-Atlantic financial and war lobbies that have controlled the world economy since the end of World War II.

I have known Mrs. LaRouche personally since the early 1980s, when I was holding some strings of power in my homeland, and I fought hand in hand with the Schiller Institute, which is an international center of thought (think-tank), and participated in its scientific and political seminars in Washington, Paris, Rome, Düsseldorf, and many other cities. I had at the same time an intellectual and friendly relationship with Mrs.

Southwest Asia

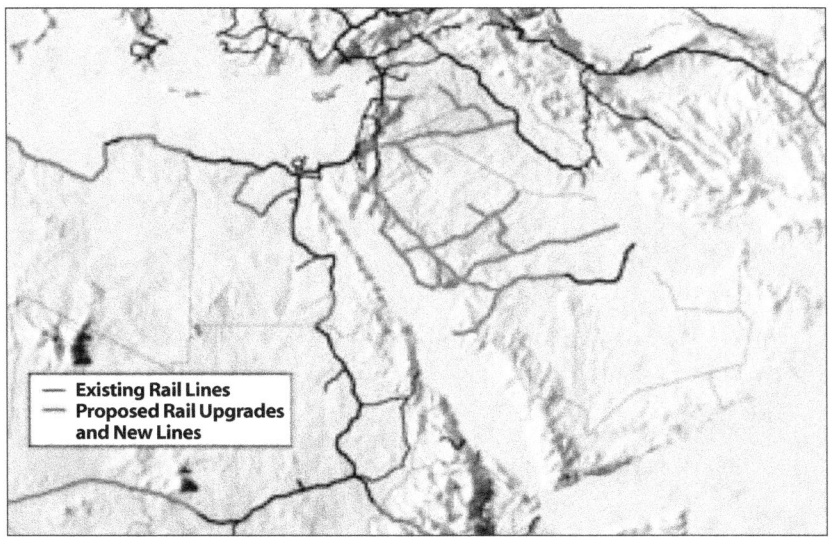

Existing Rail Lines
Proposed Rail Upgrades
and New Lines

EIRNS

LaRouche and her husband, Mr. Lyndon LaRouche, the economic advisor of former President Ronald Reagan, and was often invited for lunch or dinner in their residences in the U.S.A. and in Germany. Mr. LaRouche is American and Mrs. Helga Zepp-LaRouche is German, and they brought together America and Europe in one bond through their long struggle for the New Silk Road and the belt of economic development. My friend, the Iraqi intellectual Hussein Askary, and I, have been the only two Arabs fully committed to these principles and values to this date. And today, I feel joy and pride that these principles have finally achieved victory after three full decades.

Second, I rejoiced this week over the participation of his excellency the Minister of Transportation of Qatar in the Belt and Road Forum in Beijing, upon the recommendation of His Highness the Emir of Qatar.

Third, I received a gift this week from my friend Hussein Askary—the new book, published recently by *EIR* with the title *The New Silk Road Becomes the World Land-Bridge*, in an Arabic version translated by Askary. This is a gigantic book, which presents the details and the intentions of the alternative world order, through detailed maps, precise numbers, clear projects, and the facts of multinational agreements and commitments— making the reader fully aware of the truth that the dream which we had in the 1980s is now transformed into a practical program and an applicable mega-project that is capable of transcending borders, ideologies, political

conflicts, and the remnants of sectarian and ethnic struggles, and overwhelming the whole of mankind, with its blessings, through an international network of true solidarity and means of transcontinental communications.

In this book (of which privately donated copies have been sent as gifts to hundreds of prominent Arabs through their embassies), the public can read how security and peace can be established among nations with the tools of international cooperation, especially in our Arab-Islamic regions. Hussein Askary explains, in Part Six of the book, the types of connectivity projects among nations, the connections that existed before the suppressive trans-Atlantic system severed them to usher the region into the new cold war, openly threatening the world with a third, this time nuclear, world war.

These projects are:
• The **Berlin to Baghdad Railway**,
• The **Hijaz Railway** through the countries of the Middle East and the Arabian Peninsula,
• The **Orient Express**, connecting the Middle East to North Africa,
• The **Zubaida Road**, the old Kufa-Mecca pilgrims' road, from Baghdad to Najaf, Hail, and the Holy Al-Medina and Mecca,
• The **Nile Route** connecting Egypt and Sudan to the Great Lakes nations of Africa, and finally,
• The **Arab Maghreb Route** that constitutes a regional belt connecting Alexandria, Tripoli, Sfax, Tunis, Algiers, and Fez.

I truly believe that this just and alternative world order is founded on a completely different set of international relations, exemplified by the recently established group of nations, composed of China, Russia, India, Brazil, and South Africa—the BRICS.

President Trump has been considering joining this caravan and said so during his meeting with the Russian Foreign Minister, Mr. Lavrov, last week. This new world order must be the key item on the agenda of the G-20 Summit, which will be held on July 7-8 in Hamburg, Germany. We require a total mutiny against the evils of the Euro-American system that has dominated the world in the past 70 years.

The Way Out of the Crisis—The Historic Precedent of the American Colonies[1]

by Roger Moore

Money is the creature of law, and the creation of the original issue of money should be maintained as the exclusive monopoly of national government. Money possesses no value to the state other than that given to it by circulation.

> —United States President Abraham Lincoln, weeks before his assassination in 1865, justifying his issuance of government credit in the form of the Greenback currency, during the Civil War.

WIESBADEN, Germany, May 22—Approximately one century prior to the American Revolution, the German philosophical genius, Gottfried Leibniz, enunciated the first modern scientific approach to defining principles of economics based on human development. Leibniz's method was one of *physical economy*, as opposed to monetary and statistical notions of wealth. In 1671 he authored two works—*Society and Economy*[2] and *On the Establishment in Germany of a Society for the Promotion of Arts and Sciences*[3]—in which he investigates the principle that human discovery and creativity, particularly as expressed in scientific and technological inventions, form the basis of a productive economy and human progress. These two works were written just prior to Leibniz's

The Dutch-English wars made London the eventual center of power, based on seapower.

wikipedia

move to Paris, where he was to work in the orbit of Jean-Baptiste Colbert, the First Minister of State, who had led the economic revival of France.

Leibniz vs. John Locke: The Emergence of Imperial London

Gottfried Wilhelm Leibniz's first diplomatic deployment by the Elector of Mainz in 1672 to Paris, at the age of 27, ultimately failed in its explicit effort to head off King Louis XIV's war against Holland,[4] a war that resulted in a the unraveling of the 1648 Peace of Westphalia, the peace treaty which earlier had ended the savage destruction of the Thirty Years War. This unraveling, however, was not some design of the foolish French King, but a calculated intrigue by Europe's imperial monetarist faction to make London the eventual center of power for an unchallengeable world empire based on sea power.

London was assigned to gain imperial dominance over the income stream of the trans-Atlantic slave trade and to impose a "globalized" corruption on the colonies in the New World—using slave (and peon) labor for plantation-driven production of commodities, largely sugar and tobacco. Not only did Louis XIV finance an English attack on Holland, just before his own, but with his land war, he squandered the French fleet, which had

---

1. A version of this article was first circulated in 2009.

2. http://www.larouchepub.com/eiw/public/1991/eirv18n01-19910104/eirv18n01-19910104_012-leibnizs_first_writing_on_societ.pdf

3. http://www.schillerinstitute.org/fid_91-96/922_liebniz_A_and_S.html

4. See U.S. naval officer and historian A.T. Mahan's *The Influence of Sea Power Upon History 1660-1783*, p. 141: "Leibnitz proposes to Louis to seize Egypt."

---

been built up by Leibniz's patron in Paris, Jean-Baptiste Colbert, the First Minister of State. In fact, this war created such domestic turbulence in Holland that it resulted in the seizure of power by William of Orange, who later became, in 1688, King William III of England! And thus, with both the French and Dutch—the only other relevant maritime military powers in the world—suffering the results of wartime destruction and bankruptcy, London began its pre-designed ascendancy, which achieved, scarcely a century later in 1763, at the end of the Seven Years War, unchallenged imperial supremacy of the entire world. The Anglo-Dutch imperial monetary system—a system based on monetarism, slavery, and enforced backwardness—now had a new military (largely naval) power center, the British Empire.

Ironically, the new, Britain-based imperial system soon suffered its first defeat, with the success of the American Rev-

Pro-feudalist John Locke (top) promoted turning over the slave trade to London.

olution. The seeds of this defeat were already germinating in England's American colonies, exactly at the time that London's future imperial role was being crafted in the mid-1600s. The drive for sovereign development of the colonies, free from imperial monetarist trade and Europe's oligarchic corruption, was one continuity, including the Massachusetts Bay Colony's revolution in mobilizing *Public Credit* against private monetarism in the late 1600s, through to Benjamin Franklin's leading of colonial resistance to the Parliament of Great Britain's effort to suppress it with the Currency Act of 1764. The resulting conflict became the American Revolution.

The Netherlands had long been the main trans-Atlantic slave-trading and commercial maritime power with its Dutch West Indies Company. It is no mere co-

incidence that—in furtherance of the imperial scheme to promote London—John Locke, Leibniz's adversary, in 1672 was a co-investor along with his patron, Anthony Ashley Cooper, the Earl of Shaftesbury, in the newly founded, London-based Royal Africa Company (RAC), created to turn control of the slave trade over to London. In 1673, Locke was appointed Secretary to the Council of Trade and Plantations, which supervised the deadly triangular trade of slaves, sugar, and manufactured goods.

Locke had been no stranger to this schema, having been secretary to the proprietors of Carolina in 1663. He was also the author of the *Fundamental Constitutions of Carolina* in 1669, an infamous document promoting feudalism and slavery. The RAC was later to take over the Spanish contract for supplying Spain's new world colonies with African slaves, called the *Asiento*. The idea?—military hegemony over commodity production using globalized slave labor. It was a strictly Venetian concept: London becomes hegemonic militarily and otherwise hegemonic, and other nations and interests are relegated to the role of mere subcontractors. Today, the continental European nations of the euro currency zone still haven't learned this lesson, that they are mere subcontractors to London's control over what is left of global monetarist finance.

The American Response: Public Credit versus Private Imperial Monetarism

Discussions in the New World, in particular the Massachusetts Bay Colony and Connecticut, were directly opposed to these disasters for humanity. These American colonies focussed instead on how to finance their actual development, free from the hegemonic monetarist trading schemes reigning over all of Europe and London, trading schemes that necessitated the expansion of slave economies across the Atlantic, in the Americas.

It is a noteworthy irony of history, that out of a few "new world" English colonies, with but tens of thousands of inhabitants, there emerged states with virtually republican Charters, as in the case of the Massachusetts Bay Colony, from which were to be born that United States of America, with its Constitution, which estabished the precedent for any possibility to end imperial monetarist control over sovereign nations' finance.

In 1690, Massachusetts had uttered the first Public Credit, in the form of government *Bills of Credit*, that the western world had ever seen. Alexander Hamilton, the key author of the new Constitution of the United States of America, incorporated this tradition in the new government's national bank, the First Bank of the United States.

Cotton Mather

Wikipedia
The integrated Saugus Iron Works of Massachusetts (1646).

The American colonies had continually suffered under the London-orchestrated monetarist trade system which subordinated real economic criteria to the manipulation of gold and silver coinage, and the trade deal advances (bills of exchange) of the London merchant houses. As seen in the case of John Locke, in both his authorship of the Carolina colony slave trading constitution, and in his Royal Africa Company investments, this trade system was dominated by the Caribbean-centered slave economies which were expanding into the southern colonies.

Means of credit circulation for industry, like the integrated Saugus Iron Works of Massachusetts (1646), or other manufactures and agricultural development, outside of this London monetary system and commodity trade, were non-existent. Thus arose the necessity to

use the authority of government to create Public Credit, and its monetization, for purposes of domestic economic development and trade. Were Cardinal Nicholas of Cusa alive to witness private chartered companies exploiting slave and peon labor, corrupting the New World project he had personally launched, he would have shuddered in disgust.

In the 1650s, Connecticut Governor John Winthrop Jr. (a correspondent of Johannes Kepler) had been in correspondence with Samuel Hartlib in London, reviewing one William Potter's proposals, incorporated in his *Keys of Wealth* (London, 1650), for the establishment of a Land Bank to issue Bills of Credit to landowners (farmers), which Bills would then circulate as paper money and would be given the status of *Legal Tender*, as means of payment of all contracts. John Winthrop Jr. and his father, like Increase Mather and his son Cotton Mather, were prominent 17th-century leaders of colonial America. Winthrop Jr. had written in 1660 to Hartlib that his own conception of a Land Bank could be implemented on much better terms than Potter had proposed for England, even including Hartlib's own thoughts on Potter's proposal incorporated in the Hartlib pamphlet, *An Essay upon Master W. Potters Designe* (London, 1653). During a Summer 1661 trip to London, Winthrop Jr. submitted a proposition to the Royal Society for a such a bank. A subsequent correspondence of Samuel Hartlib, which was called *Talent of the Bank of Lands & Commodities,* documents his support for Winthrop's proposal.[5]

Thus, in these first decades after the 1648 Peace of

---

5. Andrew McFarland Davis, *Currency and Banking in the Province of Massachusetts Bay*, 1901. Volume II, Chapter IV.

Isaac Newton, a monetarist, was deployed to the Royal Mint 1696.

Westphalia, the soul of what had been best in England and throughout Europe was already transferred to the American colonies. The Bank of Venice and the Venetian-inspired Dutch Bank of Amsterdam (1609) were by then already hegemonic in Europe, and their monetarist methods were much discussed among London's Lombard Street goldsmiths, the city's proto-bankers of the day. This Venetian tendency took control and eventually created the imperial "dream team" of John Locke and Isaac Newton, who concretized the Venetian "reforms" of 1694-1696 under the Anglo-Dutch reign of Queen Mary and William of Orange (of Holland) of 1688 "Glorious Revolution" infamy. In 1696, Locke and Newton were deployed, Locke to head the Privy Council's new Board of Trade (controlling trade with the colonies), and Newton, to the Royal Mint, for the new monetarist coinage reform. This effort followed the founding of the Bank of England in 1694 to service private financial interests.

But, just prior to this, the Massachusetts colonial assembly used the unsettled conditions in England—after William of Orange's 1688 invasion of England—to overthrow the colony's Royal Governor Andros in 1689. Andros had stopped a short-lived Land Bank experiment in 1688 and voided all land titles, returning ownership to the Crown. In 1690, as described by Cotton Mather in his *Magnalia Christi Americana*[6] and

his 1691 pamphlet "Some Additional Considerations on the Bills of Credit Now Passing in New England ...," the elected assembly then uttered and distributed paper Bills of Credit to pay returning militia members involved in a failed military operation against the French in Canada. These Bills of Credit then, in turn, served for further use as generally accepted paper currency (monetization). Cotton's father Increase Mather was in London at this time, fighting for the return of Massachusetts' republic-style Charter, which had been nullified by London in 1686.

Cotton Mather's 1691 pamphlet defended this revolution against the London "hard money," "intrinsic value" practices dominating the London trade system, which only functioned to drain the colony of coinage and wealth. He describes the process of the General Court of Massachusetts (the elected assembly) uttering Public Credit which becomes paper currency:

> What is the use of coyned silver? but to furnish a man with Credit, that he may obtain from his Neighbours those Commodities, which he hath occasion for? The Country in General Court, have Recognized or Acknowledged, a Debt of so many thousand pounds unto them that have been the servants of the Publick. The Credit conveyed by the Bills now Circulates from one hand to another as mens dealings are, until the Public Taxes call for it. It is then brought in to the Treasurers hands, from which it goes not out again. Now the Conveniences which the servants of the Publick, have had by them, have honestly paid the Countries Debts; and what could coyned Silver have done more?

In 1692, according to State of Massachusetts archives, the colony mandated

> that all Bills of publick creditt, issued forth by order of the General Court of the late Colony of the Massachusetts Bay, shall pass current within this Province in all payments equivalent to money and all publick payments a 5 per cent advance.

This 5 percent tax cut, upon paying taxes with the paper Bills of Credit, was designed to stabilize their value and use in normal private trade within the colony. Withdrawal of the paper Bills of Credit and continual

---

6. On pages 190-191 of the books.google.com scanned 1855 edition, one finds Cotton Mather's account of the issuance of the Bills of Credit.

re-issuance by the assembly made them the key factor in domestic trade.

By the early 1700s most of the colonies had introduced Bills of Credit to facilitate their economic development. The Bills of Credit, issued for government purchases, were often accompanied by Assembly-created Land Banks (also known as Loan Banks or Offices). They too would issue paper Bills of Credit as loans with interest, secured by the borrower's land as security, which the borrower would circulate as paper currency. According to Professor Richard Sylla in the *Journal of Economic History*:

One can almost visualize a logistic diffusion curve as the Bay Colony's bills were emulated by South Carolina (1703), New Hampshire, Connecticut, New York, New Jersey (all in 1709), Rhode Island (1710), North Carolina (1712), Pennsylvania (1723), and Maryland (1733). The other three colonies eventually made use of the technique. A closely related innovation was the loan office (or land bank or loan bank, as it is sometimes called). Colonies organized these "banks" to lend bills to individual borrowers with land as security. South Carolina led the way in 1712, followed by Massachusetts (in 1714), Rhode Island, (1715), New Hampshire (1717), Pennsylvania and Delaware (1723), New Jersey (1724), North Carolina (1729), Connecticut and Maryland (1733), New York (1737), and Georgia (1755).

These were not Venetian-style banks, and they did not follow the oligarchic methodology of lending out money accumulated as deposits for usury by private financial cartels. They were part of the Assembly-enacted credit system built around government uttered Bills of Credit. As the Governor of Pennsylvania wrote about the 1723 Loan Office utterance of £45,000 of paper money loans, at 5 percent interest, with no more than 100 pounds to a person:

Benjamin Franklin (left) fulfilled the legacy of Cotton Mather (right) and John Winthrop, Jr.

The poor middling People who had any Lands or Houses to pledge, borrow'd from the Loan-Office and paid off their usurious creditors; and to render them more easy for the future, as well as to bring Things nearer to Par, lawful interest was reduced at this Time from eight to six per Cent, by which means the Town was soon filled with People, and Business all over the province expanded at a great rate.

Benjamin Franklin Fulfills the John Winthrop Jr. and Cotton Mather Legacy

In 1720, London imperial authorities sent out circular instructions to colonial governors demanding they suppress the Bills of Credit, and by 1726, the British Lords of Trade and Plantations threatened to appeal to the King to repeal Pennsylvania's acts *"if any further Acts [were] pass'd for creating more Bills of Credit"* to circulate as money. In 1729, a 23-year-old printer, Benjamin Franklin, established himself as the theoretician of this ongoing practice, when he penned an essay in support of the Pennsylvania Assembly issuing new Bills of Credit: "A Modest Enquiry into the Nature and Necessity of a Paper-Currency."

After the death of his aging acquaintance Cotton Mather in 1728, Benjamin Franklin emerged as the leading figure—the champion—in defense of the colonies and their Public Credit system, a role he maintained for five decades straight through to the Revolution.

London repeatedly sought to end the colonies' sovereign act of Public Credit utterance. Acts of Parliament, Royal Decrees, and Board of Trade directives were all utilized to force colonial Royal Governors to crack down on the assemblies which authorized the Bills of Credit. In 1743 Massachusetts governor William Shirley (or one of his supporters) wrote a defense of the Bills of Credit entitled, *An Enquiry into the State of the Bills of Credit of the Province of the Massachu-*

setts Bay of New England.[7] It followed a bitter battle in the Bay Colony around the Land Bank effort of 1740, which was suppressed by Parliament and London's colonial agents. Economic warfare by manipulating specie and trade with the colonies could be used to devalue the circulating Bills of Credit. Like the post-U.S. Civil War "specie resumption" effort, this "hard money" campaign was used to force withdrawal of the Bills of Credit, and Great Britain delivered to Massachusetts gold and silver specie in payment for colonial military expenses, but, with IMF-style "currency reform" conditionalities attached.

Benjamin Franklin met scientist Abraham Kästner (shown here) in Germany in 1766.

The resulting Massachusetts Currency Reform Act of 1749, imposed on the province, began so:

> An Act for drawing in the Bills of Credit of the several Denominations which have at any time been issued by this government and are still outstanding, and for ascertaining the rate of Coin'd Silver in this Province for the future.

Following these measures to crush Public Credit in Massachusetts, on June 10, 1751, the Parliament of Great Britain enacted the Currency Act of 1751, extending the war against Public Credit to all New England colonies. It began with the following heading:

> An Act to regulate and restrain Paper Bills of Credit in his Majesty's Colonies or Plantations of **Rhode Island** and **Providence Plantations**, **Connecticut**, the **Massachusetts Bay**, and **New Hampshire** in America; and to prevent the same being legal Tenders in Payments of Money.

Although the French and Indian Wars (Seven Years' War, 1756-63) made it possible for the colonies to continue issuing Bills of Credit for military expenses, this issue of sovereign Public Credit for the purpose of the physical development of the colonies increasingly emerged at the center of Benjamin Franklin's subsequent efforts to organize the Revolution. With the end of the Seven Years' War, Britain had attained global maritime and military supremacy. Following the Treaty of Paris in 1763, the private British East India Company became the cornerstone of the British Empire. When the Parliament of Great Britain enacted the Currency Act of 1764, that Empire promptly began an aggressive effort to suppress the actions of the American colonies. This act extended the Currency Act of 1751, imposing an imperial prohibition on the further issuance of legal-tender paper currency to all the other colonies. Franklin's reaction was immediate, and he went off to London, representing Pennsylvania, but leading the effort of all the colonies against this and related imperial impositions like the Stamp Act. This was not merely against Great Britain, but a fight against an imperial financial conglomerate which had made London its center.

In the midst of his battle in London against the Empire's effort to suppress sovereign Public Credit in the colonies, Franklin took the time in 1766 to visit Hannover and Göttingen in Germany, meeting there with Rudolf Erich Raspe and scientist Abraham Kästner. With Raspe, he visited the Leibniz archive in Hannover and presumably discussed with his two interlocutors the profound principles enunciated by Leibniz, which had been brought back to world attention by Raspe's 1765 publishing of Leibniz's long suppressed attack on John Locke, *New Essays on Human Understanding*.

From that 1766 visit by Franklin to Hannover and Göttingen, it would be but a scant half-score years until the *Declaration of Independence* was issued by the American colonies. Thus did Benjamin Franklin begin the final phase of revolutionary activities leading to the success of the American Revolution.

---

7. The full text of this history of Bills of Credit in Massachusetts, beginning in 1690, is available on the Internet at http://etext.virginia.edu/users/brock/ Enquiry.htm

'CONVICT HIM OR KILL HIM!'

The Night They Came To Kill Me

by Lyndon H. LaRouche, Jr.

This statement was issued by the LaRouche in 2004 Presidential campaign committee on March 2, 2004.

On October 6, 1986, a virtual army of more than four hundred armed personnel descended upon the town of Leesburg, Virginia, for a raid on the offices of *EIR* and its associates, and also deployed for another, darker mission. The premises at which I was residing at that time were surrounded by an armed force, while aircraft, armored vehicles, and other personnel waited for the order to move in shooting. Fortunately, the killing did not happen, because someone with higher authority than the Justice Department Criminal Division head William Weld, ordered the attack on me called off. The forces readied to move in on me, my wife, and a number of my associates, were pulled back in the morning.

That was the second fully documented case of a U.S. Justice Department involvement in operations aimed at my personal elimination from politics. The first was documented in an FBI internal document dated late 1973. The first was an internal U.S. operation; the second, of Oct. 6-7, 1986, was international, including the involvement of the Soviet government of General Secretary Mikhail Gorbachev. To understand the higher level of command behind the way in which the Democratic National Committee bureaucrats have used the Party's nullification of the Voting Rights Act to attempt to exclude me from this election, we must point to the crucial features of the 1973 and 1986 attempts at my personal elimination.

This is not only my cause for complaint. The great majority of Americans are as much the intended victim as I am. They have a right to know what is being done to them in this connection. I explain.

EIRNS/Stuart Lewis

The FBI raid on the Leesburg, Virginia headquarters of the LaRouche movement, Oct. 6, 1986. Over 400 armed personnel were deployed in the operation, whose purpose included the assassination of Lyndon LaRouche—a mission aborted by last-minute intervention from the highest level of government.

Those events of Oct. 6-7, 1986 began in Sweden, when someone killed that nation's Prime Minister, Olof Palme, and immediately, fraudulently, assigned blame for the killing action to me. That libel was promptly adopted by my long-standing, usually lying enemies at the *Washington Post*, and copied by other well-known news-media cesspools. This killing occurred in the context of a massive outpouring of preparatory hate-propaganda against me, world-wide, from the government of Armand Hammer-associate Gorbachev. The issue behind the Soviet participation in the attack, was Soviet inside knowledge of my role in introducing what President Ronald Reagan had named publicly the "Strategic Defense Initiative (SDI)." Gorbachev, like his former sponsor, Soviet General Secretary Yuri Andropov, hated me on account of my international, as well as U.S. role in the development of the SDI proposal.

It became clear in the course of that year, that the killing of expendable target Palme was used, and therefore probably intended, to set into motion an environment for what would later pass as a "justified, retaliatory" killing of me; no other plausible motive for the killing of Palme has been presented to the public, up to the present day. Tracing all the relevant developments, over both the interval from that shooting, to the Leesburg events of Oct. 6-7, later that same year, all of the relevant events in the pattern of action, including the preparatory steps taken by Boston's William Weld, represent a systemically functional connection between the killing of Palme and the referenced events of Oct. 6-7.

When those two Justice Department "elimination" operations against me are considered, the obvious question is: "Are the two actions, those of 1973 and 1986, related?" They are, in fact, closely related, and are key to understanding why the financial powers behind Democratic National Committee Chairman Terry McAuliffe's actions against me, have been so hysterically determined to exclude the one Democratic Presidential candidate who now represents, presently, officially, the broadest popular base of financial support of all current Democratic contenders. Why do the forces behind these actions fear me so much that they would take such extraordinarily high political risks in running these kinds of efforts to bring about my personal and political elimination?

In the second case, Oct. 6-7, 1986, the obvious motive for the projected official killing of me, my wife, and others on that occasion, was my role in the development of the SDI. Ironically, but not accidentally, this operation was unleashed at the time President Reagan was meeting Gorbachev in Reykjavik, Iceland, where the President, once again, firmly restated his commitment to SDI.

However, there is a direct connection to the earlier 1973 FBI operation. The 1973 campaign for my "elimination," the near-slaughter of Oct. 6-7, 1986, and the stubborn effort to exclude me from the debates now, are each and all products of the same issue of my fight against the effort of certain liberal economists, and others, to put the world as a whole under the thumb of the policies of former Nazi Economics Minister Hjalmar Schacht.

The ultimate origin of these and related actions is not the U.S. Department of Justice, but a much higher authority than the U.S. government, the same assortment of Venetian-style international financier-oligarchical interests, and their associated law firms, which unleashed the wave of fascist dictatorships in continental Europe over the interval 1922-1945. The common feature of those international financier interests, then, back during 1922-1945, and today, is their present commitment to imposing Schachtian economics upon both the U.S.A. itself, and also on the world at large, as the presently ongoing looting of Argentina typifies such fascist practices in action.

The intention of those financiers behind the demand for my exclusion from the Democratic Party proceedings, is to attempt to ensure that the next President of the U.S.A. is nothing but a pro-fascist banker's office boy in matters of national economic and social policy. A notable number of these pro-Schachtian financier interests are the proverbial "big bucks" behind the Democratic Party.

Three Linked Issues

Behind all of the operations against me, from 1973 through the present day, is a reflection of the common characteristic of three tightly linked issues. The first, my pro-FDR opposition to Schachtian economics. The second, my opposition to the so-called "utopian" military doctrines currently associated with "beast-man" Dick Cheney. Third, my intention to reverse the folly of the past forty years' downward drift of the U.S.A., from the world's leading producer nation, to today's preda-

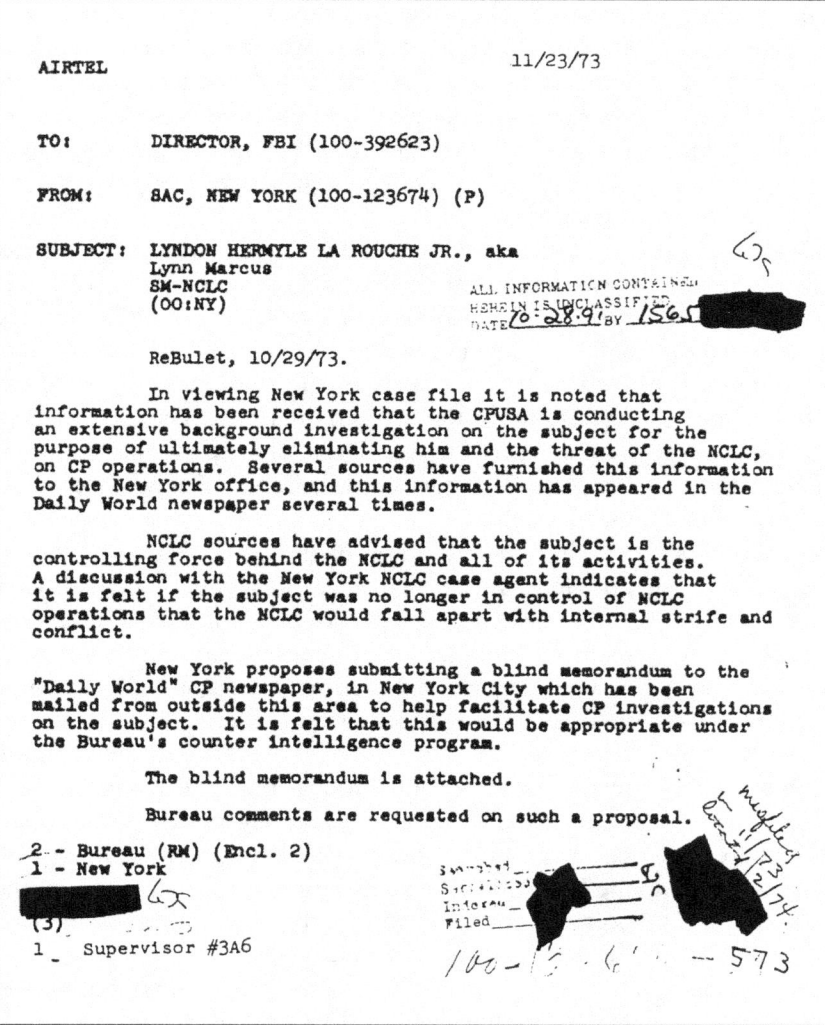

AIRTEL   11/23/73

TO: DIRECTOR, FBI (100-392623)

FROM: SAC, NEW YORK (100-123674) (P)

SUBJECT: LYNDON HERMYLE LA ROUCHE JR., aka
          Lynn Marcus
          SM-NCLC
          (OO:NY)   ALL INFORMATION CONTAINED
                                     HEREIN IS UNCLASSIFIED
                                     DATE 10-28-91 BY 156S

          ReBulet, 10/29/73.

          In viewing New York case file it is noted that
information has been received that the CPUSA is conducting
an extensive background investigation on the subject for the
purpose of ultimately eliminating him and the threat of the NCLC,
on CP operations. Several sources have furnished this information
to the New York office, and this information has appeared in the
Daily World newspaper several times.

          NCLC sources have advised that the subject is the
controlling force behind the NCLC and all of its activities.
A discussion with the New York NCLC case agent indicates that
it is felt if the subject was no longer in control of NCLC
operations that the NCLC would fall apart with internal strife and
conflict.

          New York proposes submitting a blind memorandum to the
"Daily World" CP newspaper, in New York City which has been
mailed from outside this area to help facilitate CP investigations
on the subject. It is felt that this would be appropriate under
the Bureau's counter intelligence program.

          The blind memorandum is attached.

          Bureau comments are requested on such a proposal.

2 - Bureau (RM) (Encl. 2)
1 - New York

(3)
1   Supervisor #3A6

This FBI internal memorandum of Nov. 23, 1973 calls for agency support to the Communist Party of the United States (CPUSA) in its effort to "eliminate" Lyndon LaRouche.

tory mess of Roman Empire-style "post-industrial" bread and circuses.

Go back to the late Summer and Fall of 1971. When the breakdown of the Bretton Woods system was ordered by President Richard Nixon, on August 15-16, 1971, I responded, denouncing the incompetence of those leading economists who had insisted that such an event could never happen under the so-called "built-in stabilizers." Since the mid-1960s, I had warned repeatedly, publicly, against such a highly probable trend, of a series of international monetary crises leading toward the consequent breakdown of the present world monetary system. It had happened.

Once again, I had been proven right as a long-range economic forecaster; virtually every university economics textbook, virtually every professor or similar type had been proven totally wrong on this issue.

Therefore, my associates and I launched a campaign against "Quackademic" economics professors. The turmoil this campaign produced on the campuses, and elsewhere, impelled the pained economists and their owners to select a champion of their cause, to defeat me in open debate. What soon proved to be the luckless Professor Abba Lerner, reputedly the leading resident Keynesian economist in the U.S.A., was selected for the contest.

We faced off on the premises of New York's Queens College campus. Professors and comparable notables chiefly gathered in the front rows, and students and others chiefly behind them. My challenge to Lerner was that his current proposals for Brazil were an echo of the doctrines of Nazi Economics Minister Hjalmar Schacht. I warned that his policy toward Brazil was typical of the kinds of fascist-like austerity policies which would be pushed under the new conditions created by Nixon's action. For the alloted time, and more, Lerner squirmed and wriggled, seeking to change the subject from the concrete issue I had posed as the test question of the time: Brazil policy. Then, the debate closed when Lerner whimpered, "But if Germany had accepted Schacht's policies, Hitler would not have been necessary." The assembled body reacted to this whimpered utterance as if stunned. Lerner was, figuratively, carried, *hors de combat*, from that day's field of battle.

Since that occasion, no leading economist in any part of the world has found the courage to challenge me in a debate on these crucial issues of Schachtian economic policy being pushed by the U.S. since that time. As Lerner's friend Professor Sidney Hook stated the point: "LaRouche won the debate, but"—he will lose much more as a result of that. It was his way of saying that the "establishment" would unite against me; it did.

There was no coincidence in any of this. The shift of the U.S. and British economies away from the U.S.'s leading role as the world's greatest producer nation, toward a pro-Schachtian, "post-industrial" utopianism, was the hallmark of the 1966-1968 Nixon campaign for the Presidency. The follies of this "post-industrial" shift into wild-eyed monetarism, led the U.S. government to the point, that it must abandon its foolish post-Kennedy economic and cultural policies, or make exactly the choice I had warned that I feared they would make. Nixon's decision of August 15, 1971 made the march in the direction of ruin and fascist-like dictatorship inevitable. Nixon's mid-August decision thus made the issue of the 1971 La-Rouche-Lerner debate the inevitable continuing, leading issue of U.S. economic policy, from that date to the present neo-Schachtian days of Lazard Frères-associated Felix Rohatyn.

Nixon's decision put the leading institutions and voters of the U.S. into a virtual ideological-economic fishbowl. That is to say: The poor fish might think he can rule the universe by choosing that part of the interior of the fishbowl to which he might wish to swim, but the bowl itself was being moved without his consciousness of the direction into which the bowl was being carried. Such are the sometimes tragic, utopian delusions of Cartesian and other true believers in what they define as "self-evident" definitions, axioms, and postulates. The universe in which they believe, is only a fishbowl filled with those fools who believe that their own free choice, according to such beliefs, controls their destiny.

Most ordinary people today have little appreciation of the fierceness with which pro-Schachtian liberal financiers hate the memory of President Franklin Roosevelt. Most corporate and kindred Baby Boomers, such as my rivals for the Presidency, do not even know what a Schachtian tactic is. Nonetheless, the defeat, chiefly

The assassination of Swedish Prime Minister Olof Palme on Feb. 28, 1986 "was used, and therefore probably intended, to set into motion an environment for what would later pass as a 'justified, retaliatory' killing of me; no other plausible motive for the killing of Palme has been presented to the public, up to the present day."

by Roosevelt's U.S.A., of those pro-Synarchist, pro-Schachtian financiers' effort to create a fascist internationalism during the post-Versailles decades, has prompted the financiers of today to seek every possible means to uproot and destroy the kind of agro-industrial constitutional republic which Roosevelt's victory over Hitler et al. represented. So, in August 1944, as soon as the U.S.-led breakthrough in Normandy had sealed the early doom of Hitler, those financier circles which had temporarily supported Roosevelt's war-effort, launched the right turn represented by Bertrand Russell's leading role in putting forward a utopian strategic doctrine of imperial world government through preventive nuclear war.

During his two terms in office, military traditionalist President Dwight Eisenhower defended our constitutional order from the rampaging utopians he labelled a "military-industrial complex." President John F. Kennedy's assassination broke the back of the resistance to those utopians; the U.S. official plunge into the quicksands of asymmetric warfare in Indo-China, and the parallel, mid-1960s "post-industrial" shift, were the concomitant of that victory of the utopians. The murders of Martin Luther King and Bobby Kennedy, were crucial elements of the march toward ruin of our economic culture, and worse, beyond.

The mid-1960s' cultural-paradigm down-shift, merely typified by the dionysiac rock-drug-sex counterculture, was the destruction of the mind and gut of what had been the world's greatest economy, the U.S. economy. The purpose of that induced cultural-paradigm shift was to uproot everything about the U.S. which was reflected in FDR's achievements as President.

My proposal for what President Reagan was later to name his "Strategic Defense Initiative" was prompted by a recognition of the growing actual risk of general thermonuclear war, in the doctrines of James R. Schlesinger's cabal, around the theme of the "present danger." I reacted out of my conviction that the nuclear madness of Trilateral Brzezinski's cronies, Schlesinger et al., showed that the U.S. must find ways to engage the Soviet Union in a long-term alternative to the thermonuclear war implicit in a continuation of the Russell-like, so-called "détente" policies of the 1970s. Thus, when the Reagan National Security Council entertained my back-channel discussions with the Soviet government, to explore what I proposed as the relevant alternative, I became a grave danger to the policies of the utopians inside and outside our defense establishment. At the close of the President's televised address of March 23, 1983, they decided I was too capable a political force of opposition to their schemes to be allowed to live. It is the same issue I represent against Cheney and his pack of neo-conservative lunatics today. That was the principal motive behind the indicated events of 1986.

In this way, the issue of my opposition to Schachtian economics, to utopian military madness, and to the past four decades' cultural-paradigm down-shift of the economy, mind, and morals of our nation, are three aspects of the same issue. For that, they wished me "eliminated" in 1973, sought to eliminate me by shameless open actions in 1986, and wish to eliminate all traces of my international influence today.

'Prison, Anyone?'

The abortion of the shooting assault intended for Oct. 6-7, 1986, led to a subsequent, high-level, intense debate in relevant circles. "Shall we kill him, or imprison him?" was the tenor of that debate. The threat from the utopian faction was, "If you allow him to beat the legal frame-up we are conducting, you will not stop us from killing him this time!"

That decision was in debate from no later than the evening of President Reagan's televised address of March 23, 1983. After a few days, the utopians had regrouped their forces around circles including the right-wing utopian, and fervent SDI (and LaRouche and Edward Teller opponents) Daniel P. Graham and the utopians of the Heritage Foundation. So, the name of SDI was continued, but, under the influence of circles backing Graham, the content was changed radically to emphasize obsolete, chiefly "off-the-shelf" technologies of no use for the indicated type of mission-assignment.

On Oct. 12, 1988, I delivered a memorable address in Berlin, which was taped there for later broadcast, that same month, on a nationwide TV campaign feature. I forecast the imminent collapse of the Soviet alliance, beginning probably soon in Poland, and spreading into other parts of Eastern Europe and the Soviet economy itself. I proposed a course of U.S. action to deal, through affirmative economic action, with the opportunity to uproot the embedded institutions of major military conflict throughout the world.

I was soon hustled off to the hoosegow by the fastest, if perhaps the most crooked railroad in the U.S.A., the Alexandria Federal Courthouse in the Eastern District of Virginia. So, in effect, the newly sworn President George Bush put me into prison, and, a little more than five years later, Bill Clinton pulled me out. Now, the world makes a new turn around the circle of crisis. This time, those bankers who wish to put a Democrat who would be a virtual office boy for their Schachtian policies into the White House, are at it again. They are terrified at the thought that I, no office boy in these matters, would come even close to the White House.

Some leaders of nations are elected, others are either killed, or sent to prison to be defamed. So, powerful financier cabals have often ordered the fate of nations and the people, if the people let that happen. Thus, in today's world, the ultimate feat of importance for a republic, is to get competent leaders elected, and keep them from being killed at a sign from the hand of a pro-Synarchist financier mafioso.

II. LaRouche on Education

The Inner Workings of Alma Deutscher's Musical Genius

by Michelle Rasmussen

I want to write beautiful music—music that makes the world a better place.
—Alma Deutscher

May 19—When I think about 12-year-old Alma Deutscher, the budding English composer, violinist, and pianist, I cannot help but be reminded of Robert Schumann's first public statement about Frédéric Chopin: "Hats off, gentlemen, a genius."[1]

Our political movement is dedicated to the proposition that all children can become geniuses, if their creative potential is developed. Alma is proof of that. We are convinced that the most important challenge of humanity is to develop a strategy to unleash the creativity of every man, woman and child, and that a crucial method to achieve this, is by reliving the creative discoveries of the past. Alma is also proof of that. And we are determined to create a new global renaissance, for which new musical compositions, based on the principles of the greatest classical music, will help lead the way. Again, Alma's young musical mind and soul already prove that it is possible.

A Very Young Classical Music Composer

On December 29, 2016, Alma's first full-length opera, *Cinderella*, had its European debut in Vienna, under the baton of Zubin Mehta, who dubbed her "one of the greatest musical talents today."[2] The reader may see a shorter version, performed in Hebrew with English subtitles, on YouTube.[3]

Alex Nightingale Smith/almadeutscher.com

"If the world is so ugly, then what's the point of making it even uglier, with ugly music? ... So, if you want to hear how ugly the modern world is, then you don't need to come to my concert in July. You can just switch on the television."

In addition to the beautiful music, Alma also rewrote the plot. The evil step-mother runs an opera company, the step-sisters are talentless divas, Cinderella is a composer, and the prince is a poet. The prince finds Cinderella because she is the only one who can sing the continuation of the song she composed for one of his poems.

Alma had previously written a short, one-act opera, *The Sweeper of Dreams*, and has also composed piano, violin, and chamber music, as well as concertos and orchestral works, many of which are available on her YouTube channel,[4] and on her CD.[5]

But, for this author, that which most reveals the inner workings of Alma's musical creativity, is hearing her

---

1. In *Allgemeine Musikalische Zeitung*, a review of Chopin's *Variations on "Là ci darem la mano"* by Mozart.
2. One aria from the Vienna performance. / Quote from Alma's new website under Reviews: http://www.almadeutscher.com/.
3. First part.
Second part.

4. Alma's YouTube channel.
5. *The Music of Alma Deutscher*, CD, mp3, Flara Records, 2013.

Rosa solemnis/youtube

Alma Deutscher greets conductor Zubin Mehta on his arrival in Vienna for the rehearsals of her opera, Cinderella. The performances, in December 2016, were sold out. It will be performed again at Schloss Kittsee near Vienna on July 12, 2017.

improvise, either alone, or in a musical dialogue with her teacher, Tobias Cramm, starting at the age of 5.[6]

Alma thinks and breaths music—beautiful, classical music, which modulates (between keys, between major and minor), develops, surprises, moves, and delights. She has developed her power of imagination to such a degree, that she can close her eyes and let her imagination develop musical ideas, while keeping the all-important *"Il Filo,"* or red thread, in mind. *Il Filo*, a metaphor used by Mozart's father Leopold, among others, is "the cognitive thread that, like Ariadne's thread which led Theseus through the labyrinth, guides the listener through a musical work."[7]

Alma has developed this special power of creating musical development bounded by a unity of effect, which the legendary Amadeus Quartet's first violinist, Norbert Brainin, and his friend Lyndon LaRouche, call "motivführung."[8]

Starting with a musical motif with pregnant possibilities, provoked by naturally developing paradoxes, the composition leaps from one discovery to the next, driven by a subsuming, generative musical thought-object. LaRouche's criterion is, "Can the Many transitions, and developments linking transitions, all be subsumed under the directing governance of an unchangeable idea of the composition as a whole?"[9] The origin of such a musical thought-object is a "divine spark of potential for rigorous forms of creative reason."[10]

During the many interviews with her, Alma is self-reflective and tries to put words to her creative process. Her musical ideas come to her when she is improvising at the piano, during an "improvising mood," but often, when she is not trying to produce them—while dreaming, just before or after sleeping, when skipping rope, relaxing, or doing something else. The melodies just flow into her musical mind. "I just hear this beautiful melody. It plays inside my mind."

But then, she says, the hard work begins, to compose the other voices that will entwine the initial melody voice, and to develop the ideas as creatively as possible.

When asked to describe the process of how she turns these melodies into a piece of music, Alma self-reflectively responded, "Lots of people think that the difficult part of composing, is, actually, to get the idea, but actually, that just comes to me. The difficult bit is to then sit down and, with that idea, to develop it, and combine it with other ideas in a coherent way. Because it's very easy just to throw a soup of lots of ideas, which don't make any sense together, but to sit down and develop it, and to combine it, and then afterwards to tweak it, and polish it, that takes ages, sometimes even years."[11]

Alma is inspired by the composers Mozart, Schubert, and Tchaikovsky—who, she thinks, have the most beautiful melodies and harmonies—and by girls like Fanny Mendelssohn, Felix Mendelssohn's sister, and Nannerl, Mozart's sister, who were extremely talented, but were not allowed to become composers because they were girls.

Alma is also inspired by other creative people, not

6. For example: Alma Deutscher (age 7) and Tobias Cramm improvising together on the organ, February 2012; Alma Deutscher (age 7), improvisation on "Hänschen Klein"; joint improvisation by Alma Deutscher and Tobias Cramm (around age 9); and "Intermezzo with Arik Vardi," Israel Educational Television, Alma Deutscher, Jan. 3, 2014. See others on her website cited above.

7. Gjerdingen, Robert. *Music in the Galant Style*. Oxford University Press, 2007, p. 369.

8. LaRouche, Lyndon. "Mozart's 1782-1786 Revolution in Music," *Fidelio*, Winter 1992. In the article, LaRouche describes the musical motivführung revolution started by Haydn, then taken to a higher level by Mozart, by integrating Haydn's discovery, with an earlier breakthrough by Bach.

9. LaRouche, Lyndon. "That Which Underlies Motivic Thorough-Composition," *EIR*, vol. 44, no. 6, Feb. 10, 2017, first published in 1995, p. 62.

10. Listen, for example, to her *Variations in E-flat major*.

11. Alma Deutscher, Composer—Violinist and Pianist—The World Around Us, ZeitgeistMinds.

only in the field of music, but also in science. When asked about her creativity, she responded:

I don't go to school. I learn at home. I'm home-schooled. I read lots of books, I love reading. ... I read biographies about scientists and composers.[12]

There is no TV. She reads books, "and imagines how it must be."
And, she is also inspired by others who made a difference: "I want to change the world too."[13]

Nourishing a Musical Genius

Alma sang before she could speak. The two-year-old Alma started playing the piano, and the violin at three. At the age of four, her parents prepared a CD for her with classical music lullabies, and the one that she loved the most was by Richard Strauss, especially because of a specific harmonic shift in the first few measures.[14] "How can music be so beautiful?" she asked her mother.

At three, Alma started improvising music at the piano, and wrote her first compositions at four. Her father, Israeli linguist Guy Deutscher, said, "The greatest moment was when we realized that she was playing her own melodies."[15] He decided to take Alma's musical soul seriously, and began searching for methods of teaching classical music composition to children—and for a teacher.

He discovered a book, *Music in the Galant Style*,[16] by Robert Gjerdingen, professor of music at Northwestern University's School of Music. Gjerdingen reveals the results of his exhaustive search through the libraries of Naples and other Italian cities to find the original sources, the pedagogical workbooks, known as *partimenti* (or singular, *partimento*, using the word to mean the method itself) of 18th-century music masters. *Partimento* was also taught to, or by, non-Italians such as Bach, Händel, Haydn, and Mozart.

Alma Deutscher/youtube

Alma Deutscher, at age 7, improvising at the organ jointly with her teacher, Tobias Cramm, in "question and answer" form—each responding to the other's contribution by turns.

For example, Joseph Haydn recorded that:

I wrote diligently but not in a well-founded way until, finally, I had the good fortune to learn the true fundamentals of composition from the celebrated Herr Porpora (who was in Vienna at that time).[17]

Nicola Porpora was educated in, and then taught in the *partimento* tradition in Naples.

In the 18th Century, Italian children living in "conservatories," or homes to "conserve" (provide for) orphans, or poor children, were taught musical composition as a trade, by music masters, with *partimenti* as a guide.

The first step was to learn *solfeggi*, or studies in melody, in which the children would begin to learn counterpoint by singing, and listening. They would sing soprano melodies, always accompanied by a keyboard instrument, which would play the bass and, most probably, other voices. In this way, the children would start their journey toward immersion in the world of polyphony (multiple voices).

Then, it was time for *partamenti*.

---

12. "British Child Prodigy's Cinderella Opera Thrills Vienna," BBC News.
13. She also plays the violin in opera productions. "I go to a summer camp in Salzburg, where we put on an opera with some members of the Vienna Philharmonic. That's a lot of fun. This year it was *Fidelio*, and I was the concertmaster. I have a lot of friends there who play instruments."
14. "Wiegenlied," Op. 41, no. 1, from a D-major triad D-F#-A-D, to a D-E#-G#-B (followed by a C#), which we have referred to as containing "double Lydian" dissonances between D-G#, and E#-B.
15. "CBS This Morning," Dec. 27, 2016.
16. Gjerdingen, Robert. See note 7.

17. Diergarten, Felix. "'The True Fundamentals of Composition': Haydn's Partimento Counterpoint," *Eighteenth-Century Music*, vol. 8, no. 1, March 2011, pp. 53-75. This article shows how the *partimenti* tradition influenced Haydn, using several of his fugues as examples.

"In a sense, *solfeggi* and *partimenti* (instructional basses) were two sides of the same polyphonic coin. *Partimenti* provided a bass to which the student added one or more upper voices in a keyboard realization. ... Thus the melody-bass duo at the heart of eighteenth-century music was taught and reinforced from both the top and the bottom,"[18] or, as in another description, a "musical *pas de deux* [ballet duet] of *solfeggio*-melody and *partimenti* bass."

With the aid of *partimenti*, the children learned how to discover the unseen and unheard "missing" three voices above a given bass melody, that is, the soprano, alto, and tenor voices, to create a full, four-voiced polyphonic composition. "*[P]artimento* was but one voice in a virtual ensemble that played in the mind of the student and became sound through realization at the keyboard."[19]

Partimenti were not limited to the bass line, however, and there could be clef changes. Giorgio Sanguinetti, another leading *partimenti* researcher, provides this definition: "A *partimento* is a sketch, written on a single staff, whose main purpose is to be a guide for improvisation of a composition at the keyboard."[20]

As Gjerdingen stressed in an interview, the primary focus was not vertical chords, but developing the facility to improvise horizontal voices—four independent voices that would weave a beautiful, developing tonal carpet—the essence of counterpoint.

The student also learned to recognize commonly used musical building blocks, with which they could enrich their powers of imagination, needed to realize the given *partimenti* line (play the other voices), improvise impromptu, or compose new works. Gjerdingen writes:

> Viewing *partimenti* as traces of a lost culture of music training, one can see that while *partimenti* did provide students practice in keyboard accompaniment, harmony, and counterpoint, the more talented and devoted students also gained a rich training of the musical imagination. One might say, without too much exaggeration, that for the eighteenth-century court musician, *partimenti* were a mode of musical thought. Today the *partimenti* provide a window into the musi-

cal world of that time, and they can still help train young musicians who want an insider's understanding of this great musical heritage.

The German Version of *Partimenti*

The Italian *partimento* was similar to, but not exactly the same as the German *Generalbass*, known in English as figured bass or thoroughbass. During the 17th and 18th Centuries, the distinction between composer and performer was much more fluid than today. Musicians were expected to be able to improvise four-voiced counterpoint, given only a bass voice, sometimes with and sometimes without small numbers associated with some of the notes, indicating musical intervals above the bass line—a series of vertical clues that the musician used to improvise the other horizontal voices.

Johann Sebastian Bach said:

> Figured bass is the most perfect foundation of music. It is executed with both hands in such a manner that the left hand plays the notes that are written, while the right adds consonances and dissonances thereto, making an agreeable harmony for the glory of God and the justifiable gratification of the soul. Like all music, the figured bass should have no other end and aim than the glory of God and the recreation of the soul; where this is not kept in mind there is no true music, but only an infernal clamor and ranting.[21]

Bach's first biographer, Johann Nikolaus Forkel, in his chapter, "Bach the Teacher," wrote:

> Bach's method of teaching composition was as sure and excellent as his method of teaching how to play. He did not begin with dry counterpoints that led nowhere, as was done by other teachers of music in his time; still less did he detain his scholars with the calculations of the proportions of tones, ... He proceeded at once to the pure thorough bass in four parts, and insisted particularly on the writing out of these parts, because thereby the idea of the pure progression of the harmony is rendered the most evident.
>
> He then proceeded to chorales [hymns]. In the exercises, he at first set the basses himself and made the pupils invent only the alto and

---

18. "Solfeggi in Their Historical Context."
19. "Partimenti in Their Historical Context."
20. Sanguinetti, Giorgio. *The Art of Partimento: History, Theory, and Practice.* Oxford University Press, 2012, p. 14.

21. Schweitzer, Albert. *J.S. Bach.* Vol. 1, p. 167.

Alma Deutscher/youtube

Alma Deutscher was the soloist when her own violin concerto was performed by the Israel Philharmonic Orchestra, when she was 9.

Thus we have solid documentation that both Bach and Händel utilized thoroughbass to teach composition to their students.

Alma's Teacher

Gjerdingen told Alma's father, Guy Deutscher, that there was no one teaching the *partimento* method in Britain, but pointed him in the direction of Tobias Cramm, who studied at the University of Basel, Switzerland, and is currently a music teacher at the Musikschule Laufental-Thierstein in Laufen, Switzerland. Alma has been taking lessons with Cramm via Skype! Their keyboards are connected, to enable them to improvise together in a fascinating way, each playing a phrase, which provokes a response from the other. They call it "Question and Answer."

(This author has been engaged in a very fruitful "Singing Question and Answer" improvisation game process with the very musical seven-year-old son of two Schiller Institute colleagues, after the three of them had started playing it. We alternate starting off, and it is fascinating to hear how much his singing responses cohere with the opening statement, how he responds directly to the preceding phrase by the other and to the jointly developing melodic and/or rhythmical theme. Some examples are available on the website of the Schiller Institute in Denmark.[24])

Cramm's teacher was Rudolf Lutz, organist at St. Laurenzen church in St. Gallen, Switzerland, who is one of the foremost improvisers in the style of Bach. He is also the artistic director of the J.S. Bach-Stiftung (J.S. Bach Foundation), which is in the process of recording all of Bach's vocal works.

Alma's father also plays a role in facilitating her composing. Sometimes he helps her write down her musical ideas, and advises her if he thinks some parts of her composition are too boring. Alma also sends her compositions to Gjerdingen for advice.

tenor to them. By degrees, he let them also make the basses. He everywhere insisted not only on the highest degree of purity in the harmony itself, but also on natural connection and flowing melody in all the parts. Every connoisseur knows what models he has himself produced in this kind; his middle parts are often so singable that they might be used as upper parts.[22]

The great composer Georg Friedrich Händel has bequeathed to us his own teaching exercises, which enable the reader to learn how to "realize" the given thoroughbasses, and also, thoroughbass fugues. Fugues, both learnéd (more elaborate, worked out on paper) and thoroughbass (improvised), are the epitome of counterpoint. The lessons that Händel wrote to teach the daughters of King George II and his wife Caroline, herself a collaborator of Leibniz, have been published as *Continuo Playing According to Handel: His Figured Bass Exercises.*[23]

22. David, Hans T., and Mendel, Arthur, eds., *The New Bach Reader: A Life of Johann Sebastian Bach in Letters and Documents*. Revised and expanded by Christoph Wolff. New York: W.W. Norton, 1998, p. 454. Bach's own rules of thorough bass are included at page 206, although Bach ends by saying that the other precautions to be observed are better explained in oral instruction. If only we had had recording equipment at that time!

23. *Continuo Playing According to Handel: His Figured Bass Exer-*

cises, with a commentary by David Ledbetter. Oxford: Clarendon Press, 1990.

24. Singing Question and Answer with Alexander Gent Gillesberg and this author.

Classical Music or Modern?

Alma said, in a 2016 interview with the German daily, *Die Zeit*, "Modern music I find annoying. It's noise that hurts my ears. I prefer to listen to beautiful melodies. ... I love to write beautiful melodies and beautiful harmonies, and I mix in my melodies harmonies used by different composers."[25]

She has also transformed her teacher's view about composition in our time. *Die Zeit*'s interviewer: "What is innovation in music? Previously, Alma's teacher Tobias Cramm thought that serious 'classical' music must sound contemporary, must therefore be 'modern classic,' otherwise it would be pure imitation. But he says that he has learned better. One can be creative even with the tradition. Alma revives the old language again, and 'her tunes accompany me.' "

The interviewer asks, "Alma, what is your main goal?" Alma responds:

I want people to love classical music again, not just listen to pop music. There should be more real composers again, like there used to be. I want to change the world, to make it more beautiful.

In conclusion, the author will leave you with a more in-depth personal statement by Alma about what she is striving to accomplish. It is from a video she made for the Feb. 21, 2017 press conference held by the Carinthian Summer Music Festival in Austria. Alma will hold a concert there on July 16, consisting solely of her own compositions. She says:

I want to tell you something important about my music in general, about my style, and my musical language, about what's the point of music. Some people have told me that I compose in a musical language of the past, and that this is not allowed in the 21st Century. In the past, it was possible to compose beautiful melodies and beautiful music, but today, they say, I'm not allowed to compose like this anymore, because I need to discover the complexity of the modern world, and that the point of music, is to show the complexity of the world.

Well, let me tell you a huge secret. I already

know that the world is complex, and can be very ugly, but I think that these people have just got a little bit confused. If the world is so ugly, then what's the point of making it even uglier, with ugly music?

Alma then tells the story, recounted here, of hearing Strauss' lullaby and asking her parents, "How can music be so beautiful?"

Soon after that, I started to invent my own melodies, and in all the music I have composed since, I have always tried to make it sound as beautiful as I can, otherwise, what's the point? Maybe I can't do it as beautifully as Strauss, but I'm trying.

So, if you want to hear how ugly the modern world is, then you don't need to come to my concert in July. You can just switch on the television, and listen to the news. But I think that most people actually go to concerts because they want to hear beautiful music—music full of melodies that you can hum or sing, music that speaks to the heart, music that makes you want to smile, or cry, or dance. There's enough ugliness in the world. I want to write beautiful music—music that makes the world a better place."[26]

Well, Alma, you have actually already done that. Of the some four million people who have seen Alma's YouTube videos, many have left written comments that express that the beauty that you, who are so young, have created for them, has brought tears of joy to their eyes. You have given us the hope that all children can become geniuses, if only they can be allowed to develop their creative potential.

To LaRouche, classical music, displayed in "a domain of empyreal beauty," in the mind, not the senses, is an "indispensable spiritual nourishment of the agapic creative powers of reason."[27] You, Alma, have given us the hope that the lost art of classical music composition, may not be lost, after all.

Other articles on music and culture by Michelle Rasmussen may be found at http://schillerinstitut.dk/si/tag/michelle_rasmussen/.

mich.ras@hotmail.com

25. Uwe Jean Heuser interviewed Alma Deutscher in *Die Zeit*, January 7, 2016. Excerpts in translation are posted on her Facebook page at https://www.facebook.com/AlmaDeutscher/posts/487087171495436

26. www.youtube.com/watch?v=7yf_pbVvIWk
27. LaRouche, Lyndon. "That Which Underlies Motivic Thorough-Composition," p. 70. See note 9.

On the Subject of Education

by Lyndon H. LaRouche, Jr.

The following policy-statement was released by La-Rouche's Committee for a New Bretton Woods, the principal campaign committee for Lyndon H. LaRouche Jr.'s bid for the Democratic party presidential nomination in 2000.

The function of this policy-statement is, both, to define the goals which the Federal government must set for public education, and, also, define the means and methods which the Federal government, especially its Executive Branch, should employ to promote those goals which were implied in the Preamble of the Federal Constitution of 1789. I emphasize a policy for education which is axiomatically consistent with "the general welfare clause."

Most of today's citizens appear to agree, that there has been an accelerating deterioration in the performance of primary and secondary education, since the middle of the 1960s. Unfortunately, many of the more popular, proposed remedies for this problem, are cures worse than the disease. More and more of our citizens have been lured, some out of desperation, into various kinds of "cure-all" "home remedies" and "patent medicines" for the ills of our schools. Any among such proposed changes would have the effect of destroying what little good presently remains among the shards of our nation's predominantly ruined primary and secondary education.

Among my duties here, I shall identify the folly of the more popular of the proposed types of "quick fix-it" remedies. However, my principal task is to define a national educational policy which reverses the terrible destruction wrought upon our public school systems, to uproot those combined, perverted novelties and ruinous budget-cutting measures, which have been introduced since Club of Rome co-founder Dr. Alexander King's Paris OECD study of 1963.[1]

1.0 Division of Labor Between Federal and State Governments

As your President, my budgetary approach to needed national reforms in education, will be modelled on the post-World War II successes which the Hill-Burton Act achieved in the area of hospital and related efforts of combined Federal, state, and local government and private enterprises.[2] This is the approach I have reported, repeatedly, in addresses and in published replies to questions from journalists and others.[3] Here, I describe those principles of education which this approach is intended to serve.

Although the principles of education must be those which educate a future citizen of our constitutional republic in a manner required by the nature of our Federal republic, the greater part of the day-to-day administration of the schooling of the population, should be administered either by the Federal states, or under standards set by each of them for this purpose. Primary and secondary education is to be conducted chiefly by public institutions of the states and their localities; there, the majority of primary and secondary education should remain. If existing public educational programs are inadequate or otherwise defective, that condition should be remedied, not employed as a pretext for undermining the principled reliance upon public primary and secondary education for meeting the common requirements of educating a qualified citizenry.

That much is a matter of implicitly constitutional principles. From the beginning of our republic, even as early as the policies of education associated with the Winthrops and Mathers of the Massachusetts Bay Colony, or the circles of James Logan in the Common-

---

1. See Mark Burdman, "The NATO Plan to Kill U.S. Science," *Fusion*, Sept. 1980, pp. 41-47.

2. "Why U.S. Health Care Must Return to the Hill-Burton Standard," *EIR*, July 29, 1994.

3. E.g., "Hill-Burton Health-Care Standards," *EIR*, March 15, 1996, p. 30; "LaRouche on Health Care," *New Federalist*, Aug. 23, 1999, p. 5; "LaRouche Conducts Campaign Dialogue with Legislators," *EIR*, Oct. 1, 1999.

EIRNS/Stuart Lewis

"If existing public educational programs are inadequate or otherwise defective," LaRouche writes, "that condition should be remedied, not employed as a pretext for undermining the principled reliance upon public primary and secondary education for meeting the common requirements of educating a qualified citizenry." Shown here, a youth orchestra in New York City.

wealth of Pennsylvania, our founders were guided by a federal principle: Ours is a nation composed, constitutionally and historically, of respectively sovereign Federal states, bound together as a single Federal sovereignty, bound so by common consent to submit to rule by a community of anti-oligarchical, republican principle.

This principle is sometimes falsely represented as a "social contract." The notion of a "social contract" was rejected in the 1776 Declaration of Independence. The authors of that declaration adopted the specific language of Gottfried Leibniz, "life, liberty, and the pursuit of happiness," echoing thus Leibniz's attack on the immorality of John Locke's pro-slavery dogma of "life, liberty, and property," the latter the same Locke dogma echoed in today's use of the cult-phrase "shareholder value." This pro-Leibniz, anti-Locke conception of natural law, was later affirmed to be the supreme and permanent constitutional law of this republic, in the Preamble of the 1789 Federal Constitution. The sovereign authority and responsibility for the rule of all of the land according to that principle, reposes in the Federal government; but, the implementation of the principle in local matters should be assigned, as much as is practi-

cable, to state and local governing and administrative authorities, or left to the choice of the individual citizens.

In matters of education, as otherwise, the authority of the Federal government must protect the principled rights of the individual citizen, wherever and whenever the state government should be unwilling, or lack the means to secure those rights, including the right to a quality of education due to each and every citizen. However, whenever the state or locality has the means, competence, and disposition to care for such matters of principle, the accomplishment of that intended purpose, were better undertaken by local initiative.

As the relative success of Hill-Burton shows, the role of the Federal government in caring for matters of the general social welfare, should be first in readiness, but last in line. It must be prepared to ensure that principled objectives are realized, but must act as the strategic reserve deployed, used only when needed. The best-functioning primary and secondary public education programs and institutions of the past, such as the Philadelphia high school established under the influence of Alexander Dallas Bache, are models of this, the same Bache who was key in the establishment of the U.S.

Naval Academy, a Federal public institution of higher education, at Annapolis, Maryland.

On the level of colleges, universities, and other institutions of higher studies, we should continue the frequent practice of thirty years ago and more, to foster an assortment of Federal, state-directed, and private institutions established by and regulated under law. However, at all levels in education, both the Federal and state governments must continue to recognize the useful role contributed by those certain private primary and secondary institutions, such as parochial schools, which are willing to satisfy certain adopted common standards for a curriculum and classroom methods based upon Classical approaches employed for the purpose of fostering the cultivation of what I, among others, have defined as the creative powers of the individual student.

Notably, on this latter point, my policy is opposed to certain other Presidential candidates, such as Governor George W. Bush, in their expressed preferences for the kind of rote-learning better suited to training of either hamsters in spinning cages, or, for awarding university degrees to lazy and virtually illiterate young louts from the ranks of the idle and useless.

Thus, the challenge of rebuilding the shattered and decayed public and private educational institutions of our republic, presents the Federal government with a challenge, in the field of education, like that which the U.S. Congress addressed in the field of health care, at the time the Hill-Burton legislation was enacted.

The interdependency among the roles and efforts of sundry governmental and private educational institutions, parallels the challenge presented by our nation's hospital-care requirements institutions. The successes of Hill-Burton, prior to the catastrophic effects of the New York City municipal budgetary crisis of 1975, thus represent a model which may be the most appropriate administrative tactic for deployment of Federal budgetary resources in the rebuilding of not only our nation's shattered heath-care system, but also the wrecked educational system of today.

Moreover, the functions of protecting and promoting our nation's labor force, protecting its health, and educating both our future and young citizens, are among the most closely related features of our Federal government's consitutional imperative for promoting the general welfare. All involve close collaboration among sundry public and private institutions. Usually, the method in which the Federal government should define its responsibility in these areas, should be either the same method, or nearly the same.

In such matters, an effective method to be chosen by the Federal government, requires that in adopting laws and administrative procedures in aid of education, we must avoid and abhor those evils of a radical positivist's mentality, which inhere in a snarled, precedent-ridden clutter of purely positive law. What is to be preferred, in all legislation, is clear definitions of applicable principle, definitions rooted transparently in natural law. In all matters bearing most directly upon the general welfare, we should take special care, that we craft both legislation and administrative systems and procedures in such a way, that each specification follows coherently from a clearly stated, governing, subsuming set of principled objectives. Hill-Burton, set forth in a few pages of clear, and demonstrably most efficient statement of intent, typifies such excellent design of primary legislation.

2.0 How Our Educational Systems Were Destroyed

Make a simple test of the implicit, constitutional principle of education of our republic. How many recent graduates of U.S. secondary education, could understand the writings which won a majority of English-speaking North Americans to support both the 1776 Declaration of Independence and the 1789 adoption of our Federal Constitution? Many today could not even follow the words; more would have little or no comprehension of the issues which defined the American patriots' quarrel with the English tyranny of William of Orange, or the British monarchy of George I and his successors.

In a directly related issue: At the close of World War II, there was a trend toward increase of the amount of higher education per capita, for not only World War II veterans, but also their progeny. Unfortunately, that improvement was accompanied by a dilution of the quality of the higher education supplied; there has been, thus, an accelerating collapse in the quality of the content of public and private secondary and higher education, that even in the circumstance that the quantity and grade-level of education provided was increased. Thus, the secondary-school education of the 1930s and 1940s tended to become the university undergraduate curriculum of the 1960s and 1970s.

This erosion began with a corrupting simplification

Beginning during the 1960s, "the poisonous spread of irrationalist existentialism, spread from the Germany of Bertolt Brecht, Theodor Adorno, Hannah Arendt, Karl Jaspers, and Nazi philosopher Martin Heidegger, or such Heidegger followers as France's Jean-Paul Sartre and Frantz Fanon, struck both public and university education, with disastrous effects."

of the content of education, during the immediate post-war period. The influence of radical-positivist and existentialist instruction and textbooks, was already increasing during the late 1940s. The destruction of scientific competence which has led into the technologically catastrophic effects of "benchmarking" and scientifically illiterate doctrines of "mathematical modelling" today, established their grip on public and university education as early as the late 1950s. That and related changes in education, already being introduced during the late 1950s and early 1960s, laid the foundations for such effects as the "O-ring" catastrophe of the 1980s Shuttle program, and underlie the increasing pattern of technical failures in the U.S. aerospace field, generally, today.

Thus, the disasters we introduce to the education of our students today, will haunt us twenty to thirty and more years down the line, if we allow them to continue to be inflicted upon the children and grandchildren of those who were childhood or adolescent students during the Eisenhower, Kennedy, and Johnson years.

Until the late 1960s, the erosion in the quality of public and university education, was disguised by a trend for increase of the quantity of education, notably at the so-called "multiversity" levels. From the middle through late "Vietnam War" 1960s, there was an acceleration of wildly anti-science radicalism among those university students most strongly influenced by the "rock-drug-sex youth-counterculture." The poisonous spread of irrationalist existentialism, spread from the Germany of Bertolt Brecht, Theodor Adorno, Hannah Arendt, Karl Jaspers, and Nazi philosopher Martin Heidegger, or such Heidegger followers as France's Jean-Paul Sartre and Frantz Fanon, struck both public and university education, with disastrous effects.

The effects of a 1971-72 change from a healthy form of the old Bretton Woods system, to the disastrous, "floating-exchange-rate" system of today, was followed, inevitably, by such effects as an erupting, permanent, and worsening budgetary crisis at the Federal, state, and local levels of government. Epidemic political-economic follies, such as "post-industrial" utopianism, wildfire deregulation measures, the willful lunacies of Federal Reserve Chairmen Paul Volcker and Alan Greenspan, and wild-eyed ventures such as the Garn-St Germain and Kemp-Roth legislation, savaged the basic economic infrastructure of the U.S.A., and gutted the agro-industrial base upon which the earlier successes of our national economy and social-welfare systems, including the nation's health and educational systems, had depended absolutely.

The rampant positivism and existentialism, as expressed in the "suburbanite" voting and public-opinion trends of the recent thirty years, combined with the effects of the savagery done to our national economy, during the same period, have produced a situation typified by a collapse in the quality of what had been our better educational institutions. That better quality, as represented in New York City and elsewhere during the 1960s, has been ripped out of the institutions. During the same period, the quantity of educational support provided to the children and adolescents of the nation has also been destroyed, in the greater part.

The physical collapse in both quantity and quality of education, is aptly typified by the recent decades' elimination of competent courses in U.S.A. and European history from our secondary schools. The result is the victimization of the students, by the kinds of doctrines associated with the irrationalism of the Nazi philosopher Martin Heidegger, he the notorious, existentialist co-thinker of such avowed enemies of truthfulness as Hannah Arendt and Karl Jaspers.

Relative to the schools of thirty years ago, today's typical student is pushed out of civilized life, into a feral state of de-socialization, a state which Heidegger defined as "thrown-ness." The satanic quality of violence, which has lately erupted within so-called "white, middle-class" schools, as in the Littleton massacre, is the natural outgrowth of the influence of the kind of existentialist outlook, imported to the U.S.A. from the notorious "Frankfurt School" circles of Weimar and Nazi Germany.

In civilized society, Heidegger's doctrine is not to be fostered, otherwise it will not long remain civilized society. In civilized society, the humanity of all persons is located in the transmission of the individual experience of discovery of validated universal physical, and other principles, from past generations into the relived experience of the present generation. "Socialization," in any meaningful sense of the term, means a cultivated sense of the goodness existing in all individual persons, that to be recognized as a quality which sets each apart from, and above the beasts. That quality is the capacity to relive the discovery of validatable universal principles from the contributions of many generations of persons who have preceded us.

This definition of "socialization," as I shall clarify that here below, is the fundamental principle upon which the educational policies of the U.S. were based, in good times past, and which must be reassumed as governing policy, once more, today.

Most of us must be able to recall some moment during one's childhood, at which the idea of "death" was first impressed upon us. I mean the "idea of death," as distinct from the mere sense-perception of a death. It was a moment at which we first grasped that death was not a calamity which happened to strike some people, but that death is a virtually inevitable consequence of having been born. The idea of death is not a sense-impression, but, like all true ideas, a discoverable universal principle. It is a matter of principle, not mere sense-impression, to know that birth and death are equally part of individual life. If we were fortunate, our reaction to that saddening discovery of a universal truth, was not pessimism, not despair, but, rather, a higher form of optimism. The same optimism is characteristic of the moral benefits of good education.

In former times, until some point during the recent thirty-odd years, all happy children expressed their optimistic view of life in such forms of expression as a bright-eyed, smiling, "When I grow up, I am going to..." This idea was usually associated with the idea of education, either by reference to actual education, or an implicit reference to the gathering of knowledge by means of which the prospective adult profession might be achieved. Our optimistic view of such matters, even as children, was the fact that we had begun to relive discoveries which had been bequeathed to us by discoverers who had lived long ago.

Good teachers helped. The good teacher was the one who made the deceased historic figure come alive in one's mind, prompted one to relive a moment of discovery by that historic figure. It was as if that moment from the living mind of that historic figure had been brought back to life in oneself. There were teachers like that, and there were knowledgeable people, family guests, or hosts, who shared the same kind of moment of knowledge with a child. I gobbled up such moments;

they made me happy and optimistic about life and death, and mankind in general.

Once a child has recognized that he or she has re-lived living moments of discovery from each of many historic figures, especially discoveries of ideas which approximate a universal principle, the universe becomes a nice place in which to be born, to live, and ultimately to die. The connection to past and future, in terms of such ideas about universal principles, gives a sense of permanence to our brief visit to this thing we experience as human life. The New Testament parable concerning the talents, is especially attractive to the child who has come to view ideas in that way. You wish to become the visitor who passed through here, delivering some needed good in a timely fashion. Thus, one hears the child's voice: "When I grow up,..." Hearing that child's voice in that way, might inspire one to become a good teacher, or to become the discoverer who delivers the needed good in some timely fashion.

This optimistic view is fairly identified as "Socratic." That is especially so for our purposes here. Optimism respecting ideas, relies upon notions of truthfulness and justice. How may we be certain that a moment of historic discovery which we have re-experienced, was a valid contribution at the time that that discovery was made? Was that discovery a step forward toward truth for mankind, will it be justly viewed so still, generations beyond our time? Does it represent a contribution to the power of the human species in and over the universe as a whole? Does it represent a contribution to mankind's ability and impulse to cooperate in ways which bring about needed increases in mankind's welfare?

If those conditions are satisfied, then our view of all humanity is a loving one in the sense Plato gives to the Greek term *agapē*, the same sense which the Christian Apostle Paul emphasizes in Chapter 13 of his first letter to the Corinthians. That practiced view of humanity, past, present, and future, insofar as we experience that view within ourselves, is the basis for historical optimism respecting humanity in general, and our own existence as well.

What then, if we take that quality of optimism away—as the positivists and existentialists do? What if we introduce the pathological pessimism of Hobbes, Locke, Nietzsche, or Heidegger? What if we introduce Immanuel Kant's denial of the existence of knowable truth, as the existentialists Jaspers, Arendt, and Heidegger, among others, do. What if we accomplish this by ripping the principles of truthfulness out of education, and replace truth with the moral relativism of "sensitivity of feelings," or simply the allegedly "democratic" authority of all differing opinion, instead? The result of such uprooting of the foundations of optimism, is to turn children into adolescent and adult beast-men. That has been the cumulative effect of the last two generations of systemic demoralization of our educational systems. Another generation continued in this same direction, would assure the at least temporary elimination of all we might fairly describe as "civilized life."

Such is the aspect of education, on which the role of education in fostering the development of the moral character of the young individual depends. This is the vital aspect of U.S. education which has been virtually destroyed by the wicked changes which have evolved during the recent thirty-odd years.

It is to be emphasized again, that Nazi Heidegger's notion of "thrown-ness," is typical of the thinking of the "Frankfurt School" circles generally, and is expressed also in the bestiality of Bertolt Brecht's "Silenus cries," his dionysiac, left-Nietzschean poetry and drama. Heidegger's theme is a variation upon the "each in war against all," of Thomas Hobbes. Just as John Locke served the Confederacy as the philosopher of slavery, the same radical empiricism of Paolo Sarpi followers Francis Bacon, Thomas Hobbes, and John Locke, typifies that English-speaking variety of mind-set, which supplies the fertile ground for the growth of the closely related traditions of Bonapartism, the Confederacy, and endemic American fascism. For such a mind-set the followers of Adorno, Arendt, Jaspers, and Heidegger have a natural affinity. In the educational systems of a republic, such fascist-tending mind-sets should be examined rigorously, as a medical student must study diseases, but not propagate them.

3.0 Why Classical Education?

The dominant themes of public education, in all the good times and places of our national experience, have been, first, what a pro-Classical-Greek tradition defined as Classical knowledge in art and science, and, second, the study of history from that Classical standpoint in art and science. The two points, the Classical method and history, are closely related. The very name of public education, should mean nothing different than an education based upon such a union of these two.

EIRNS

"Schools must not be places of learning, in the way a circus animal learns to perform. Schools must be places of knowing, as a qualified scientist knows, by reliving the experience of original discoveries represented by those experiments on which truthful definitions of universal physical principles depend." Here, a performance by the Schiller Institute Chorus of Sonora, Mexico.

the ground addressed by Beard and his like. Today, matters are far, far worse. In fact, most of what is currently written, in today's mass media and elsewhere, or even said in the U.S. Congress, about the history of the U.S.A., about the crucial issues of political conflicts among our population, is usually a pack of contemptible falsehoods, or even sheer spur-of-the-moment concoctions.

The most general goals of a desperately needed reform in U.S. public education, are the fostering of both even mere literacy and a literate knowledge of actual U.S. history, and of world history, from the standpoint of the European re-discovery of America, of the founding and the development of the English-speaking colonies, of the American Revolution of 1776-1789, and of the victory against the British monarchy's asset, the Confederacy, the victory led by President Abraham Lincoln during our Civil War. These are fairly identified as the basic prerequisites of the transition from child and adolescent, to adult U.S. citizen. Such literacy is the lawful prerequisite for the powers rightly entrusted to the individual adult citizen.

What I have just said, on the interrelated subjects of literacy, history, and citizenship, contains some specific and principled implications for U.S. policies governing the methods, as well as the content of public education.

First, equality in citizenship requires meeting those standards for all pupils; no child shall be deprived of access to a quality of education conforming to those standards.

Second, the pupil must be guided into knowing what that pupil himself, or herself is talking about. The pupil must not be encouraged in the delusion that the way to know the meaning of words, is to look those words up in a dictionary, or on the Internet. To meet that second requirement, schools must not be places of learning, in

To understand the present, a citizen must know the substance of our nation's, and civilization's past. Otherwise, the discussion of the so-called issues of the U.S. Declaration of Independence and Federal Constitution, becomes degraded to arbitrary, ignorant speculations, even meaningless banter. Without the kind of secondary education in history, which was once considered obligatory in respectable secondary schools, the student's view of our nation's foundations, is degraded into the nominalist's illiterate interpretation of mere words and phrases, into a mere jumble of words spoken with little or no comprehension of what those words have meant in the sweep of U.S. history, from the early English-speaking colonies, to the present. More recently, the standard of literacy has departed the concern for truth, and has replaced truthfulness with so-called "sensitivity" to the irrational "feelings" of other persons.

Admittedly, the doctrines of historian Charles Beard were perniciously influential during my student years; but, at least, they were the kind of misinterpretation of history sufficiently imitative of rational thought, to impel me, as a secondary-school student, to reexamine the way a circus animal learns to perform. Schools must be places of knowing, as a qualified scientist knows, by reliving the experience of original discoveries represented by those experiments on which truthful definitions of universal physical principles depend.

Today's greatest single obstacle to even rudimentary comprehension of the issues of educational policy, is that for most living adults in the U.S.A. today, the central issue of a competent educational practice, is not even known to exist. That issue is the nature of the fundamental difference between mere learning and actually knowing. Usually, as in the educational proposals emanating from Texas Governor and Presidential pre-candidate George W. Bush, the incompetence of the would-be maker of educational policy, is rooted in blindness to his or her own ignorance of the subject-matter which he deludes himself into believing he or she is addressing.

Perhaps it would be an arbitrary assumption, to propose that the current popularity of a specific form of illiteracy known as belief in "mathematical modelling," is the source of the incompetence inhering in Governor Bush's declarations on the subject of public education. Whatever the source of the Governor's ignorance of that subject-matter, the ultimate effect of his blunder is about the same as if he were a true believer in the current cult of so-called mathematical modelling.

Once the citizen grasps the fundamental distinction between science and mathematical modelling, the citizen will at least have begun to grasp the nature and importance of the fundamental difference between what beasts can do, learn, and what beasts can not do: actually know. Only human beings are capable of knowing. Our children and adolescents are human, and therefore not properly subjected to the forms of training better suited to pets, cows, crows, and grizzly bears. The function of public education, is to cultivate the pupil's innate potential for knowing, rather than to induce the pupil to learn to perform mathematical or other mere tricks on command, as in periodic standard examinations.

Therefore, I focus now on the illustration supplied by a very elementary, but very important issue of physical science. This is an issue which should have been mastered by every graduate of a secondary school today: the discovery of the principle of "least time."

I use that case here, to illustrate what is meant by a validated universal physical principle. I then emphasize that that word, "idea," should be limited to identifying the class of notions which have the same character and authority as the act of discovery of a validated universal physical principle, such as "least time."

After that, I show that Classical art-forms, such as Classical poetry, Classical tragedy such as that of Aeschylus, Shakespeare, and Schiller, and Classical plastic art, such as that of the scientist-artist Leonardo da Vinci, represent true ideas generated by the same, Socratic method of actually knowing, as are validated universal physical principles.

The lie, that art is merely a matter of personal preferences in taste, or that artistic trends are reflections of the influence of some mysterious spirit of change, is a popular lie today, but a lie all the more. The Classical principle in artistic composition, is the principle of truthfulness. This means truthfulness in the same sense that validated discoveries of universal physical principles are truthful.

That much said, I indicate how the methods cultivated in the Classical science and Classical-artistic classrooms, are to be applied, to cultivate those skills which are indispensable for qualified statesmen and qualified ordinary citizens alike.

3.1 The Principle of Least Time

To illustrate the difference between mere mathematical modelling and real physical science, go back to Seventeenth-Century Europe, to the work of Johannes Kepler, who was the founder of modern astrophysics and original discoverer of the principle of universal gravitation. Then, from that standpoint, examine the work on the principles of "least time," by later geniuses strongly influenced by the successive work of the scientific pioneers Nicholas of Cusa, Leonardo da Vinci, and Kepler, such as Desargues, Fermat, Pascal, Huyghens, Leibniz, and Jean Bernouilli.

Those discoveries led, in turn, to the related discoveries by Gauss, Fresnel, Ampère, Wilhelm Weber, and Riemann. That series of successive development of the principle of least time, which became known as relativistic physics, is a process of ongoing discovery, which continues on the frontiers of physical science today. The principle of "least time" is truly elementary, and also truly revolutionary in character. It is one of those ideas which can, and must be re-created within the mind of every secondary pupil in competent secondary schools today.

I have, therefore, chosen this example, both to illustrate what the standard of secondary education must be, and to illustrate what we should agree to recognize as the act of knowing an idea.

The crucial issue, then and now, is this. Does action in the universe naturally follow the pathway of the shortest distance, as a simple-minded, and wrong notion of geometry would suggest? Fermat showed an anomaly which indicated that light does not follow the pathway of the shortest distance, but rather of the shortest time. Huyghens, following Fermat, designed an experiment which showed that the quickest time of travel, under gravitation, from A down to B, is not the shortest, straight-line pathway, but a longer, curved pathway, a curved pathway corresponding approximately to a curve known as a cycloid. The same lawful pathway was proven, by Leibniz, Bernouilli and others, to determine the path of refraction of light according to a universal principle of least time.

Later, Fresnel made a discovery which destroyed the false theories on light by Isaac Newton, and also the still popular but foolish notions of such pro-Newtonian contemporaries of Fresnel as Poisson, Coulomb, et al. Fresnel collaborator Ampère made similar discoveries for electromagnetism. Gauss, Weber, and Riemann proved the validity of Ampère's discovery. Weber's experimental proof measured the first experimentally defined electromagnetic constant, within the range of the sub-atomic scale.

In the course of the Seventeenth, Eighteenth, and early Nineteenth Centuries, this line of discoveries resulted from Leibniz's original discovery of the calculus, based on the same principle of least time. Leibniz gave this discovery of principle a more general form, as his "principle of universal least action." Gauss, whose work includes direct contributions to creating the U.S. Coast and Geodetic Survey, was, up to the present time, the world's greatest modern mathematician, and a leader among the original discoverers of what is called a "non-Euclidean geometry," or "hypergeometry." Gauss's student, Riemann, was the first to give a generalized form, freed of all arbitrary axiomatic assumptions of mathematical formalism, to hypergeometry. There, the frontiers of microphysics and optical biophysics lie, still, today.

All of these discoveries, including Leibniz's discovery of the calculus, and Gauss's revolutionary discoveries in the elementary principles of mathematics itself, were based on physical experimental evidence, not mathematical deduction.[4] No validatable universal physical principle was ever discovered, or could have been discovered, by the kinds of deductive methods used for so-called "statistical" and other kinds of simply mathematical modelling.

Now, contrast this standpoint in the history of modern physical science, to that of the so-called "mathematical modeller." The basis for the education of all secondary pupils in the rudiments of competent modern physical science, depends upon making this distinction not only clear, but making that a matter of a discovery actually experienced by each such student.

The radical school of Twentieth-Century mathematical modelling today, is typified by the corrupting influence of Bertrand Russell and such Russell acolytes as Norbert Wiener, the putative co-founder of the cult of "information theory," and radical-positivist mathematician John von Neumann. This cult has ancient roots, including the Eleatics and Sophists of ancient Greece's culture, and the English empiricist school of such followers of Venice's Paolo Sarpi as Francis Bacon, Thomas Hobbes, and John Locke. Competent secondary teachers should know these distinctions clearly, and be able to make those distinctions the actual knowledge of the secondary pupils.

That influence of Sarpi was continued under the direction of a nasty Venetian gentleman known as the Paris-based Abbot Antonio Conti. Conti, who died in 1749, created both the notorious Voltaire and the chiefly mythical English reputation of Isaac Newton. Conti orchestrated the Europe-wide, Eighteenth-Century, Romantic "Enlightenment." It was professed "Cartesian" Conti, who prompted most of the anti-scientific frauds which have persisted, as "generally accepted classroom mathematics" dogma, since Eighteenth-Century Europe, down to the many among the present-day secondary-school and university classrooms and textbooks. The root of that hoax known as popular modern theories of mathematical modelling, is to be traced, in

---

4. Reference in Bernard Riemann, "On The Hypotheses Which Underlie Geometry," *Über die Hypothesen, welche der Geometrie zu Grunde liegen,* **Bernhard Riemanns Gesammelte mathematische Werke,** H. Weber, ed. (New York :Dover Publications reprint edition, 1953), p. 288: "This leads us into the domain of another science, the realm of physics, which the nature of today's proceedings [mathematics] does not allow us to enter."

modern times, to the influence of Sarpi, Conti, and the far-flung networks of intellectual salons which those two Venetian gentlemen established during their respective, ill-fashioned lifetimes.

In its simplest expression, the cult of mathematical modelling begins, with arbitrary blind faith in the belief, that geometry, and mathematics in general, must be based upon the assumption that all space-time is "self-evidently" extended in straight-line directions, and that a straight line is the shortest, and therefore the quickest distance between any two points in pure space-time. Added to this, is the false belief set forth by the notoriously thuggish Leopold Kronecker and elaborated in Russell's **Principia Mathematica**, the delusion that mathematics can be derived from an elementary beginning in the simple comparisons made in terms of the counting numbers.

The cult of the so-called "new math," as popularized in schools during the late 1950s and 1960s, is a reflection of such simple-minded—and also very destructive—forms of mathematical blind faith. These popularized delusions, are the assumed basis for the authority of the practice of "mathematical modelling" today.

Now, look at the simple classroom apparatus which was used to demonstrate Christiaan Huyghens' original notion of the way gravity demonstrates a principle of "least time"[5] [**Figure 1a**]. Concentrate on the fact that this simple experiment confronts us with experimental evidence, demonstrating that a straight line is not the quickest distance between two points in a constant gravitational field. Already, with that experiment, the cult of "mathematical modelling" was in very deep trouble. After that work of Huyghens et al., no responsible, scientifically literate secondary school, or creditable university, could ever be excused for attempting to indoctrinate pupils in the "ivory tower" cult of linear "mathematical modelling."

This experiment is not yet a conclusive and comprehensive demonstration of a universal principle of least action, but is already a warning to schools, teachers, and parents: never fall into the delusion that science is a product of mathematics. What this experiment illustrates, is the fact known to Classical Greece, from

---

5. Christiaan Huygens, *The Pendulum Clock or Geometrical Demonstrations Concerning the Motion of Pendula as Applied to Clocks*, trans. by Richard J. Blackwell (Ames: Iowa State University, 1986).

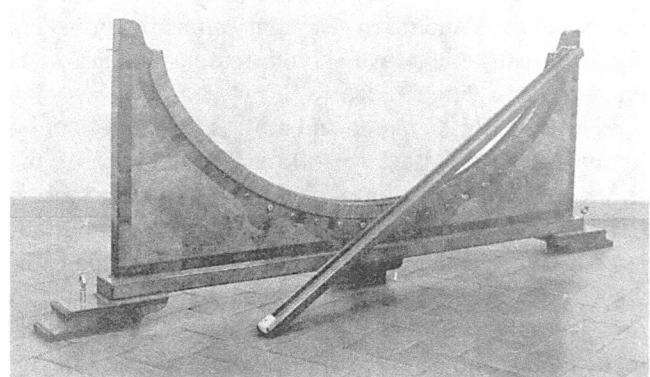

(a) A brachistochrone model built by Franesco Spighi in the 17th Century. A ball that rolls down the cycloidal track reaches the bottom faster than one rolling down the straight track.

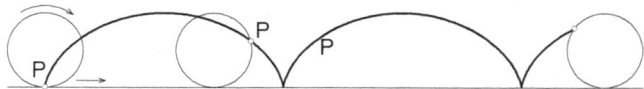

(b) The cycloid is the curve traced out by a point on a circle, as the circle rolls along a line.

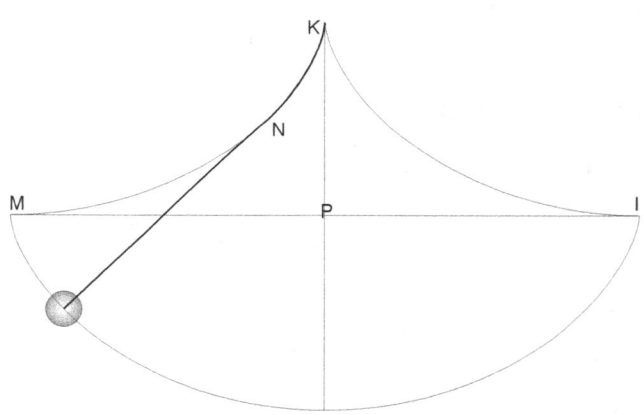

Huyghens used the cycloid to make a pendulum clock, because no matter how wide the swing, the time of the swing remains constant.

Thales and Pythagoras, through Eratosthenes, that competent mathematics is a by-product of physics, not the other way around.

So briefly consider the experiment itself. The apparatus represented in both the photo and the diagram, is to be described as follows. The experimental apparatus presents us with two tracks, side by side; one track is a straight-line track, the other a curved track. Both tracks begin and end at common points. Thus, two balls, released simultaneously along each of the tracks, can be compared for the time each ball takes, to fall its constrained pathway of distance, from the top to the bottom of the apparatus. Always, the ball travelling the longer, curved track, reaches the bottom quicker. If this demonstration holds up for other tests of the same principle, then we have demonstrated, experimentally, that the universe does not operate according to a rule which assumes that a straight line is the quickest, or even the shortest distance between two points within a real universe.

The curved track in that experiment corresponds to a curve known as a *cycloid*. You may generate a cycloid by placing a point on the outer edge of a circular wheel, and rolling the wheel along a straight surface. [**Figure 1b**.] The cycloid is a curve which is companion to another curve known as a "sine wave"; Fresnel overturned Isaac Newton's doctrine of light by showing, experimentally, that the normal pathway of propagation of light, is not in simple straight lines, but as transverse waves typified by sine waves. After the demonstrations of "least time," for light, by Leibniz and Jean Bernouilli, Ampère's, Gauss's, Riemann's, and Weber's successive contributions to the establishment of the elementary principles of electromagnetism, are a continuation of the same principle of Leibnizean least action applied by Fresnel to refute Newton's theory of light, by conclusive experimental demonstrations.

Actually, the pathways of quickest and least action in the universe are not simply cycloid pathways, but involve more complex considerations of what are known as non-constant curvatures, as such curvatures are typified by the Kepler-Gauss orbits of our Solar system. That takes us into the area of Gauss-Riemann hypergeometries. There lies the physical and mathematical significance of the notion of a "curvature of physical space-time." In other words, that means the characteristic curvature of a pathway of least action in any designated, specific kind of physical-space-time manifold. Nonetheless, those complexities aside, the demonstration of Huyghens' principle of his pendulum clock, when seen as precedent for the Leibniz-Bernouilli proof of the "least time" principle in refraction of light, is sufficient to illustrate the point I am making on education here.

That point is the following.

3.2 Present-day Follies in Scientific Education

The point is, that experience often confronts us with evidence which contradicts some belief we had earlier assumed to be unshakeable. Among the simplest illustrations of the relevant principle of education, are experiments which show the absurdity of such habits, as believing that the universe operates "self-evidently" in straight lines.

In all such cases, the solution to the crisis of belief such experiments pose, can not be found by simple deduction, such as deductive mathematics. Deduction depends upon the mistakenly assumed universal validity of certain axiomatic beliefs, upon premises such as the false, and also wrongful assumption of Leonhard Euler, et al., that the universe is extended in infinitely long straight lines, lines defined as infinitely connecting infinitesimal points. By its very nature, deductive method is, intrinsically, a method of linear analysis, or what is also known as "ivory tower" analysis; therefore, it does not correspond functionally to the real universe in which we exist.

Thus, it is in the devastating paradoxes of number theory, as shown by Carl Gauss, that a mathematics of the counting numbers shows itself to be everywhere-dense with ontological paradoxes, or, in fact, even many absurdities; Georg Cantor's, like Gauss's and Riemann's appreciation of the significance of the so-called "Sieve" of Eratosthenes, reflects this fact. The pathological element in "mathematical modelling," is axiomatically rooted in the "ivory tower" cult of deduction.

Every truly crucial experiment, like the case of the extension of the Huyghens' pendulum-clock, and other experiments, all of which led to the demonstration of a "least time" principle underlying both the refraction of light, and electromagnetism in general, overturns some part of those previously established beliefs upon which naive faith in the deductive method always relies.

Admittedly, science has often represented its knowledge, as acquired up to that point, in those terms of approximations which correspond to a linearized form of mathematical calculations. There is no fraud in the practical use of such approximations, as long as the fact that these are approximations is implicitly recognized. However, in every instance of a validated new discovery of a universal physical principle, the result is a radical overthrowing of the previously established, linearized forms of approximation practiced at the blackboard (or upon digital computer systems). In each case, as Georg Cantor appreciated the implications of Eratosthenes' "sieve,"[6] and as Nicholas of Cusa's work led to the discovery of transcendental functions, by Leibniz et al.,[7] the effect of a validatable discovery of any universal physical principle, must produce a revolutionary overturn of previously established, "generally accepted" classroom mathematics.

Simplified mathematical approximations are useful, even necessary, in their proper place. Yet, those who steer the progressive development of educational programs used in secondary schools and higher education, must be ever vigilant, never to overlook the implications of the point I have just stressed. The policy must be understood as follows.

For ordinary purposes of engineering, we usually reduce applied science to a mere approximation of truth. Frequently, thus, we use a mere approximation of truthful mathematical physics. In the practice of engineering by competent professionals, or managements of relevant government laboratories and private firms, the fact is never to be overlooked, that the mathematical models customarily used by engineers, are not science, but only a simplified approximation of the fruits of previous scientific work.

Whenever any change in technology is incorporated into design of products, or methods of production, competent professionals and managements insist upon the same kinds of experimental demonstrations which are required for validating a proposed new universal physical principle.

Similarly, public education, in its design of curricula and classroom methods, must never lose sight of the dangers inhering in a naive view of customary engineering practices.

Unfortunately, in the recent zeal for the Lockean cult of "shareholder value," both the U.S. government and leading U.S.A. and European firms have departed the pathway of sanity, into linearized "mathematical modelling" instead of science.

This cult of "mathematical modelling," was the standpoint from which the Mont Pelerin Society-controlled Heritage Foundation made a farce of what had been President Ronald Reagan's well-conceived, original proposal for a Strategic Defense Initiative. Heritage Foundation spokesman, Lt.-Gen. (ret.) Daniel Graham, was used as a Mont Pelerin Society figurehead, for insisting that "off-the-shelf" technologies of existing military contractors, not science, be the basis of ballistic missile defense. Thus, although some scientists, greatly underfunded, are still studying relevant technologies today, the official U.S. government policy on ballistic missile defense continues to be the same, worthless, and troublesome boondoggle which the Mont Pelerin Society's front, the Heritage Foundation, interjected in 1983.

Thus, today's corporate department of "design engineering" has often been transformed into a deadly economic farce, also largely under Mont Pelerin Society and related, pernicious influences, at lately increasing rates, into the mother of product-design catastrophes, that by virtue of a form of anti-scientific incompetence known variously by such names as "benchmarking," "out-sourcing," or "mathematical modelling."

Thus, the incompetence of the current Congressional proposals for "ballistic missile defense," is an example of the deadly strategic effects of simple-minded bungling in the design of products and military capabilities. It should be evident, that the incompetence shown by the recent pork-barrel programs for ballistic missile defense, reflects a toleration for incompetence in the Congress and elsewhere, a toleration which would not have been possible but for the effects of our increasingly corrupted public education systems.

For related reasons, in physical science, as in art, and in real-life history in general, the progress of human existence is always, essentially revolutionary in character. The progress of mankind's increase of power in and over the universe, is always the result of the propagation of validatable, newly discovered (or, rediscovered) universal principles. This fact is typified not only by the case of universal physical principles, but, contrary to the empiricists, positivists, Immanuel Kant, et al., also valid forms of Classical artistic composition.

"Classical" so used, includes even those folkloric artistic compositions, such as the best among the U.S.

---

6. 6. The famous "sieve" of Eratosthenes (c. 284-194 B.C.), is the starting-point from which Karl Weierstrass and Georg Cantor et al. derived their specific revolutionary contributions to modern number theory.

7. See Lyndon H. LaRouche, Jr., "On the Subject of Metaphor," *Fidelio*, Fall 1992; *Nicolaus of Cusa on Learned Ignorance*, trans. by Jasper Hopkins, pp. 52-53; Nicolaus of Cusa, "On the Quadrature of the Circle," trans. by William F. Wertz, Jr., in *Toward a New Council of Florence* (Washington, D.C.: Schiller Institute, 1995), pp. 595-610.

Negro Spiritual, whose validity is often recognized by the most accomplished Classical artists, such as Antonín Dvořák. Such folklore has the same, or sometimes even greater degree of importance, as universal principles, than many leading discoveries of universal physical principle.

It is the practice of real-life history, according to the influence of Classical progress in knowledge of universal physical and artistic knowledge, which informs the practice of society, to the effect of enabling mankind to increase its per-capita power in and over the universe, and thus its power to improve the individual human condition in a universal way. That is the standpoint of the only conceptions which deserve the name of "political science."

As the case of physical science's progress illustrates, in all discoveries of validatable universal principles, whether as science or Classical artistic composition, every such discovery of principle occurs as a creative (e.g., non-deductive, cognitive) solution for what is definable as an "ontological paradox." Such a paradox is typified by the case in which irrefutably existing evidence, overthrows the set of axiomatic assumptions underlying presently prevailing belief. In physical science, solutions to such paradoxes occur in the form of discovery of a validatable new universal physical principle. In art, as the radical discoveries in perspective, by Leonardo da Vinci, or the development of the well-tempered system of polyphony, by Johann Sebastian Bach, typify this, the notion of validatable Classical principle, is fully congruent with the notion of validatable universal physical principle in science.

All solutions to such paradoxes are generated solely by a method which is peculiar to the human mind; we call that method *individual cognition*. That method, otherwise known to Classical art and science as *reason*—as distinct from mere deduction, is the central principle of all competent policies and practices of education. Herein lies the key to recognizing the intrinsic incompetence of the recent decades' prevailing trends in public and higher education, and the often worse incompetence of what are currently proposed as remedies for the current state of education.

All competent education rests upon a grounding of the pupil's power for solving real-life problems, through re-experiencing, as faithfully as possible, the original act of discovery of a validatable universal principle, whether in science or art, a discovery effected by an original discoverer, usually one from the earlier generations, even the distant past. This aspect of public education is rightly viewed as "the cultivation of the cognitive powers of the individual pupil's mind."

Through this experience of re-enacting validatable original discoveries, the student learns to recognize, within the privacy of his, or her own sovereign powers of cognition, those non-deductive methods of thinking which occurred within the mind of the individual making some validatable discovery of universal principle, from the past.

This power of cognition, which sets the individual person apart from, and above the beasts, can not be programmed into a digital computer, can not be described at the blackboard, nor by any other expression of today's notion of "generally accepted classroom mathematics." It is known in a three-fold way.

1. It is known by re-enacting a validatable original act of discovery of a universal principle, as in reliving that experience from a creative genius of the past.

2. It is known by examining the relationship between the act of discovering, cognitively, the new principle, and the nature of the experimental, or comparable proof of the universality of the discovered, proposed new principle.

3. It is known by sharing the act of discovering and validating such an historically validated creative solution, with other persons, such as a small group of classmates and teacher. Thus, *the existence of the experience of that act of cognition, as demonstrated to exist in the mind of another person, and as shown to have a common physically-efficient expression as a result of its existence, becomes the means by which that act of cognition becomes a recognizable, and efficiently existing object of a social form of conscious knowledge.* All of the validatable discoveries of principle respecting Classical artistic composition, have the exact-same quality of certainty as socially cognizable knowledge.

This cognitive, creative potential, unique to the human individual, is not subject to observation by means of sense-perception, but it is known with certainty by the means I have indicated, nonetheless. In fact, what we know in this way, is known with a certainty which no rational person would ever ascribe to notions associated with mere powers of sense-perception of objects.

These discoveries, once known in that fashion, are what Plato defines as "ideas." The use of the term "idea," should be limited to references to validatable discoveries in the generation and application of principle. These applications are chiefly matters of scientific and Classical-artistic principles, and a political-science of ongoing history, based upon the habits of a mind which has had its cognitive powers cultivated by means of a Classical form of scientific and artistic education.

The processes of public and higher education have, thus, the following predominant functions as contributions to promotion of the general welfare.

The general function of a Classical education in mathematics and physical science, is to re-create, within the mind of each individual pupil, the original experience of all of those validated discoveries of universal principle, from the past, upon which the best practice of society today depends. This achievement, induced within each pupil, constitutes the obligation of public education to develop cultivated powers of cognition and knowledge in the minds of each and all of the graduates capable of receiving such cultivation. Persons who have assimilated and who practice such cultivated powers of judgment, are to be recognized as reasonable persons, fully qualified thus to assume the adult responsibilities of citizenship.

All young people not only have a right to access to such qualities of public education. The republic has a right to educate them in ways which ensure the future general welfare of the republic and its posterity, an education which ensures that the future citizenship shall be one of cultivated minds.

EIRNS/Stuart Lewis

"All Classical art, in contrast to 'mathematical modelling,' is based on avoidance of the untruthfulness inhering in a deductive, or so-called 'literal,' or 'dictionary' mode of argument." Here, world-renowned baritone William Warfield and pianist Sylvia Olden Lee give a class to young singers, an event sponsored by the Schiller Institute and the National Conservatory of Music Movement, in Washington, D.C. on May 11, 1996.

4.0 The Necessity of Classical Art in Schools

We do not do injustice to earlier cultures by insisting that European civilization, including that of the U.S. republic, originated within those developments in ancient Greece which are rightly distinguished as Classical today. This appreciation of the legacies of the Homeric epics, of Pythagoras, Thales, Solon, the "Age of Pericles," and of the tradition of Plato up to the time of Eratosthenes, takes into account Greek civilization's great debts to Egypt, to the Vedic, or pre-Vedic culture to which the roots of the Greek language are traced, and to the ancient transoceanic maritime cultures on which the foundations of Egyptian and Greek culture commonly depended. In speaking of Classical Greek civilization, as the founders of the U.S. republic did, we take important predecessors of Greek Classicism into account implicitly. Similarly, in speaking of the Greek Classic, we are implicitly seeking out those currents of ancient language and other heritages which we may owe to, or which we otherwise find replicated in places such as ancient China.

In all distinctions among cultures which we may find necessary to recognize, we must never lose sight of the fact that each man and woman is made equally in likeness to the Creator of the universe, and therefore a bearer of such a quality of goodness innate to all new-born individual representatives of our species. Our concern, as citizens of our anti-oligarchical republic, is to find in ourselves that expression of goodness which will be a benefit to all past and future mankind. Our national interest in this, is as Secretary of State John Quincy Adams stressed in crafting the design for President James Monroe's 1823 Monroe Doctrine: our interest as a national republic, lies in fostering a republican community of principle among the sovereign nation-state republics of this planet. All that pertains to that objective, defines our true national interest, both respecting matters internal to our republic, and in foreign affairs.

There is a quality of morality lodged within such education, which is lacking in all alternative forms of education, including most of what is often cloaked with the name of "religious instruction." The cognitive reliving of an original act of validatable discovery of principle, is not to be equated to copying a formula. In a true such cognitive discovery of principle, the person who relives an original discovery is reliving a moment from the mind of the living person, perhaps now long deceased, who made the original discovery whose experience one is replicating as a student.

In reliving many such moments, from many original discoveries, over thousands of preceding years, that aspect of humanity's past has come alive in oneself, and will be, hopefully transmitted from oneself, perhaps enriched, to persons not yet born. It is in precisely that cognitive connection of the living present to both living past and living future, that the moral quality of a cognition-centered Classical-humanistic form of education far surpasses all other modes of educational practice.

wikipedia

Hermes, by the Classical Greek sculptor Praxiteles. "The difference between the deductive formalist and the Platonist, was always the difference between the corpse and the living, the difference between the death-like symbolism of Archaic art, and the sense of life in mid-motion, conveyed by great Classical sculpture and painting...."

Persons educated in that mode become, in principle, moral citizens; persons educated in different ways, probably not so. Not all of the criminal codes and related legal means concocted could provide even a bit as much moral persuasion of a population as such a universalized Classical-humanistic approach to a universal system of public education.

It is in this aspect of a Classical-humanist mode of universal education, that the principle of cultivation of the individual mind of the future citizen comes to the fore. I now define Classical art, and Classical forms of artistic composition (as distinct, for example, from "Romantic," or "Modernist" art) from the vantage-point of the agreement between Classical artistic composition and Classical scientific method, as I have described the latter above.

In general, Classical artistic composition is to be recognized as a crucially important, integral part of that communication we know otherwise as a literate form of use of language. All Classical art, in contrast to "mathematical modelling," is based on avoidance of the untruthfulness inhering in a deductive, or so-called "literal," or "dictionary" mode of argument.

Generally, Classical art is customarily distinguished as of two general types, plastic and non-plastic. However, the underlying principles of composition of both are the same; only the mode of expression differs. Like spoken literate language, all forms of art are intrinsically social, and subject to the same tests of truthfulness or falsehood as any spoken or written prose.

Classical art lies in the recognition that any statement intended to be heard or seen as a literal, deductive copy of the referenced reality, is intrinsically a false statement, that for reason of fallacy of composition, if not otherwise. In the general case, such intrinsic falseness is of the same origin as the form of lying known as "mathematical modelling." I now present the case of Classical artistic composition from the vantage-point of defining what constitutes truthfulness in art.

4.1 'Connecting the Dots' in Art

The greatest orchestra conductor of the Twentieth Century, Wilhelm Furtwängler, described his method of conducting, as "performing between the notes." Leonardo da Vinci, centuries earlier, identified the principle of composition, in painting and plastic arts generally, to the same effect. The issue is the same I raised above, in summarizing the significance of the principle of "least time." What we define as distinct sense-impressions, may each really exist as sense-impressions, but one must not make the mistake of "connecting those dots" in a simply deductive way. This warning, against deductive modes for purporting to "connect the dots," applies as forcefully to art as it does to a mathematical form of physical science.

To make this point clear, it is indispensable that I introduce an autobiographical note of explanation here.

My own personal contribution to science came about during 1948-1952, as a result of my earlier, adolescent, pre-war attack on the *Critiques* of Immanuel Kant, that from the standpoint of the influence of Gottfried Leibniz in shaping my world-outlook.

Later, as a young man, shortly after the close of World War II, I first heard a recorded performance by conductor Wilhelm Furtwängler, while I was stationed temporarily at an army camp outside Calcutta, India. My recognition of the qualitative superiority of Furtwängler's conducting, an effect which I later identified with his use of the phrase "playing between the notes," had a profound impact, in its contribution to shaping my view of Classical artistic composition in general.

The distinctive feature of the effect of Furtwängler's conducting, was instantly clear to me. How that effect might be located in terms of the principles of polyphonic composition, was not yet so clear. Even more than a half-century later, after an intensive comparison of differences in Classical performances, I am still discovering new things bearing on that matter. Then, except for the certainty of Furtwängler's superiority over all known leading conductors, and certainty respecting the way this difference could be identified as a

wikipedia

This Classical Greek sculpture shows the Trojan priest Laocoön, wrestling with two sea serpents who kill him and his sons, after he warns the Trojans about the giant wooden horse, a gift that the Greeks have sent into their walled city.

hearable phenomenon, the effect was to drive me into a more intense re-examination of music, Classical poetry and drama, and so on, in general, than to provide settled answers to the many questions implied by such inquiries. Always, the standpoint of my inquiries was my defense of Leibniz's standpoint against the avowed irrationalism of Immanuel Kant and his like. The questioning itself bore me valuable fruit.

These and other experiences combined in effect to shape my reaction to an early 1948 reading of the Paris, paper-backed edition of Norbert Wiener's **Cybernetics**. I recognized Wiener's representation of "information theory" as a fraudulent, positivist concoction, in the same vein of axiomatic error as Kant's *Critiques*. While I chose to refute Wiener from the standpoint of the economic effect of the discovery of new physical principles, I also contrasted Wiener's lewd definition of "information" to the notion of Classical artistic ideas, as products of the same type of cognitive processes represented by valid Classical artistic principles of composition.

The outcome of my attack on the fallacy presented

Leonardo da Vinci, The Last Supper. *Careful study of this work, along with Leonardo's documentation of the principles underlying its design, "provides the teacher and students the advantage of experiencing this painting as a re-enactment of the discovery which Leonardo embodied in it. That makes the discovery itself a matter of the student's actual knowledge, rather than mere learning."*

by Wiener, was not only my original discoveries in the field of physical economy, but my including, as integral, the notion of Classical artistic principles as complementary to the discovery of validated universal physical principles. As I came to recognize that Bernhard Riemann's celebrated, 1854 habilitation dissertation, provided the key to analyzing the relationship between valid discoveries of universal physical principle and the increase of mankind's per-capita power in and over nature, I also recognized something additional. It was obvious to me, then, circa 1952, that the relations between man and nature are conditioned not only by discoveries of universal physical principles, but also the Classical form of artistic principles. That view became known later under the rubric of "The La-Rouche-Riemann Method."

Nearly five decades later, those original results, of work conducted over the 1948-1952 interval, have been rather richly cultivated by aid of practical work in many relevant fields. That is the standpoint which is reflected, inclusively, in this report "On the Subject of Education." Today, as then, that standpoint takes the act of cognition as the "fundamental variable," so to speak, which underlies all social processes. In my thus refined

use of the term "Classical," it signifies the ordering of physical scientific and artistic thought according to an all-determining, underlying role of the action and development of the human cognitive, as distinct from mere learning processes.

The way in which I approached Classical artistic composition in general, was conditioned by exposure to the quality of difference between Classical Greek sculpture and the preceding Archaic modes of Egyptian and Greek composition. Although I had not yet acquired the use of Furtwängler's description, "playing between the notes," the superiority typified by the work of Classical sculptors such as Scopas and Praxiteles, over the Archaic and the later Roman sculptors, was for me clearly a matter of the same advantage I recognized in Furtwängler's conducting of a Beethoven, Schubert, Brahms, or a Tchaikovsky symphony. For purposes of defining the principled features of Classical art, I would prefer to begin with Classical Greek sculpture as the starting-point in pedagogy.

The central issue of this presentation, the focal point, is, "How should we connect the dots?" With that focus adopted, the congruence of Classical art and science is made, quite properly, as immediate as possible.

The Classical Greek development in sculpture, as compared with the same principle better expressed in Leonardo da Vinci's *The Last Supper*, typifies the intrinsic non-linearity of the connections which Classical art, like science, makes among "the dots."

Even a preliminary sort of careful scrutiny of Classical sculpture, shows that the way in which such sculpture presents actual ideas, rather than non-cognitive forms of mere symbolism, is located in a certain irony. On the one hand, the Classical sculpture seems to portray a figure caught "off balance," and, yet, like the smile of Leonardo's *Mona Lisa*, or Rembrandt's powerful *Aristotle Contemplating the Bust of Homer*, an image of something alive, caught in mid-motion. The same is most powerfully presented by Leonardo's *The Last Supper*, especially to a visitor walking within the chapel in which it is contained. On more careful scrutiny, "off balance" turns out to be a kind of ontological paradox, which more efficiently corresponds to the reality represented than any non-Classical form of plastic composition. In this one should begin to recognize how the standard of truthfulness applies to Classical artistic composition.

For the use of secondary classroom instruction, there are functionally usable reproductions of Leonardo's *The Last Supper* available. Also useful are reproductions of Classical statues which reflect the principle associated with Scopas and Praxiteles. Reproductions of *The Last Supper* are most useful for the classroom, for several reasons. After the students have worked their way through that painting, they should seek out the corresponding specificities of Classical sculpture.

The pedagogical advantages of *The Last Supper* are chiefly of two types: first, the effect of moving in front of the painting, as if walking within the chapel where the painting is located; second, the existence of extensive documentation, by Leonardo himself, of the principles underlying the design of this painting. This provides the teacher and students the advantage of experiencing this painting as a re-enactment of the discovery which Leonardo embodied in it. That makes the discovery itself a matter of the student's actual knowledge, rather than mere learning.

Then, the teacher and students are situated to point out to one another the related principles of composition embodied in Classical Greek sculpture.

Look then at the relevant paintings by Raphael Sanzio, from this standpoint. *The School of Athens* and *The Transfiguration*, are relevant cases. Look at the bust of blind Homer seeming to examine the sightless mind of Aristotle, in the Rembrandt painting: a kind of metaphor which could not be achieved by means other than the Classical method of painting and sculpture.

4.2 Classical Music

Now, turn to music. Focus upon modern Classical thorough-composition, including the post-1782 work of Wolfgang Mozart, Josef Haydn, Ludwig v. Beethoven, Franz Schubert, Felix Mendelssohn, Frédéric Chopin, Robert Schumann, and Johannes Brahms, in contrast to their opponents, the Romantics: Rameau, Liszt, Berlioz, Wagner, Bruckner, et al. Classical thorough-composition was derived chiefly from the work and teaching of J.S. Bach. It was study of Bach's method of composition, from 1782 on, by Mozart and others, which generated modern Classical thorough-composition. Nor would pre-1782 Mozart have been possible without a Haydn influenced chiefly by a son of Bach, C.P.E. Bach.

Whence J.S. Bach—"The Bach"? The roots of Bach are very ancient, traceable from the time of Pythagoras and Plato's Academy. The proximate source of Bach's knowledge runs through the work on music by Leonardo da Vinci, who did rigorious scientific studies of vocalization, studies based on the most natural method of singing, the method associated with the Fifteenth-Century Florentine school of *bel canto* voice-training. This method, traced through Leonardo, defined implicitly six species of adult singing voices, each species characterized by a natural set of shifts in voice quality, a quality known as "registration."

The development of music, from Florence and Leonardo, shows an evolutionary development of the instruments as imitations of human singing voices and voice-registrations, and the emergence of choral polyphony and instrumental accompaniments based upon *bel canto* principles of singing. Bach's vocal and vocal-instrumental compositions, taken together with his organ works, and compositions such as his *The Musical Offering* and *The Art of the Fugue*, present us the standpoint from which Mozart launched what became modern Classical thorough-composition, as typified by Mozart's keyboard Fantasy K.475.

To appreciate the real Bach, as distinct from performances sometimes heard today, focus upon the case of two Bach Passions, the *St. John Passion* and

EIRNS/Stuart Lewis

The Leipzig Thomanerchor, during a performance in Washington, D.C. on Feb. 7, 1998. To appreciate the real Bach, LaRouche writes, imagine how his great works were performed in his day, with master soloists, a rigorously trained children's chorus, and the audience singing the chorales as responsive readings—"a far cry from attending a St. Matthew Passion as if it were a spectator sport!"

the *St. Matthew Passion*. Think of the actual performance of those Passions as Bach conventions required. We have instruments, which sing in their polyphonic imitations of specific registrations of human singing. There is a chorus of children, much like the Leipzig Thomanerchor of today. There are solists. There is the singing congregation, singing the great chorales as responsive readings. The soloists are the masters, the children's chorus rigorously trained, the well-trained orchestra, and the audience which sings as most congregations today could not! All a far cry from attending a *St. Matthew Passion* as if it were a spectator sport!

It was in this social setting, within the context of this practice of the community, that Bach developed a rigorous standard of tuning; a study of those choral works with instrumental accompaniment leave no doubt that these works could not be performed competently, unless the tuning were a well-tempered one fixed at approximately A=430 cycles.[8]

---

8. See "Keyboard Variations as Vocal Polyphony," John Sigerson and Kathy Wolfe, eds., *A Manual on the Rudiments of Tuning and Registration*, Book I (Washington, D.C.: Schiller Institute, 1992), pp. 232 ff.

This precision provided Bach the palette on which to practice his distinctive method for composing fugues, composition based upon a principle of inversions readily demonstrated to even a musically semi-literate secondary school classroom. The students will be instructed that it should be done because it is fun to do; progress toward even moderate success promotes a sense of happiness about the whole business. This refined palette gave Mozart the premise for carrying Bach's discovery forward into what became Classical methods of composition through the last great compositions of Brahms, notably featuring his Fourth Symphony and his *Four Serious Songs*.

Looking at this history of Classical composition in even that relatively restricted way, points us toward the way in which the standard of truthfulness arises in Classical musical composition: "You must not cheat!" Looking at the same matter a bit deeper, contrast Bach and the Classical composers, with so-called music which was composed like endless salami—or Germany's famous "curry sausage," such as the infinitely boring productions of Rameau: when one has already heard too much, chop it off! The characteristic of a Bach, or a later Classical composition, is that it has a natural beginning, and a natural ending—unlike the endless sausages composed later by Anton Bruckner. Serious composers were fussy about saying what they had to say: not more, nor less.

To understand how a Classical composition works, think of it as like a planetary orbit, as Kepler and then Gauss define the functional character of a planetary orbit. In both planetary orbits and Classical composition, the beginning and ending of the performance of the cycle is defined by a principle of development which is the characteristic of the orbit as an entirety. Bach's approach to the composition of fugues typifies this likeness.

The developmental principle characteristic of a Classical musical composition, is a nested set of ironies, which converge upon a single, pervasive metaphor. Each of these contrapuntal ironies, has the quality of a necessary dissonance to be resolved. One must see the dissonance in this case not as some arbitrary dissonance, but as reflecting the same principle of irony underlying the Classical method of sculpture associated with Scopas and Praxiteles, and Leonardo's *The Last Supper*. It is not dissonance in the sense of falseness, but dissonance in the sense of a true ontological paradox. Just as a validatable discovery of a universal physical principle resolves the valid dissonance we see as an ontological paradox, so a great Classical musical composition defines a subsuming musical-ontological paradox, whose solution is the identity of that composition taken as an indivisible whole.

Thus, a Classical musical composition should say that much, and not more.

One of the great difficulties standing in the way of successful musical composition, prior to Mozart's discovery, was a deadly ban on including what was termed "the Devil's Interval"—e.g., Lydian intervals—within a composition. The ban was, at best, silly superstition; but, although Bach developed the use of that banned principle, as he did in his *A Musical Offering*, for example, it was not until Mozart's so-called "Dissonant Quartet," and his prefacing of his K.475 Fantasy to his K.457 keyboard sonata, that this principle of Classical composition was openly stated as such. See Mozart's *Ave Verum Corpus* for a compact and beautiful example of this.

In the composition of Classical works, and in their performance, the crucial thing is to follow Furtwängler's rule of performance: "performing between the notes." Like keeping a planet safely on track, the essential thing in any Classical musical performance, is never to depart from submission to the developmental conception which is the pervasive characteristic of the composition taken as a whole. This requirement, as it is met in the conducting of Furtwängler, typifies the difference between the performer who plays the composer's music, rather than the pedant or bungler, who prefers to play the mere notes of the printed score. Think of notes as "dots." In Classical composition, the music does not lie in the dots, but in the connection which the dots are intended to reflect: hence, "playing between the notes."

The worst performers are those who treat the transitions in music as separations, like the links between the salami on a string. The artist treats these apparent separations as functionally connections, as the transitions which reflect the characteristic developmental ironies of the composition as a whole. Compare Furtwängler's recorded direction of a London performance of Schubert's Ninth Symphony with that of almost any other conductor; the difference is almost overwhelming!

4.3 Music and Poetry: The Principle of the Verb

Although vision is the dominant sense, singing and hearing song are the dominant expression of social relations. Language which is sung, or, in other words, vocalized, is called poetry, but only under certain conditions. The characteristic of Classical poetry is what is called metaphor, signifying ideas as I have defined the use of the term "idea" above. That much can be stated, and taught, with a large, and, indeed, profound degree of certainty. If one attempts to show the rules of use of language, but with reference to some ancient very-early development of language, much idle speculation tends to pollute the discussion.

Thus, review the nature of some of those difficulties which lure the incautious into wild speculations. Where shall we draw the line between arbitrary speculation and evidence, in efforts to trace the pre-historic development of what we know as language today?

There are certain difficulties in the way of attempting to trace the origins of even the presently known language families. Any attempt to assess the probable origins and functional characteristics of the early development of language, must rely on methods which might be less than obvious to the layman, but nonetheless permit us to draw certain firm conclusions concerning the lawful development and more effective forms of use of languages. In addressing the closely related aspects of poetry and music, the indicated difficulties must be taken into account.

The difficulty in assessing certain of the pre-historic origins, and presumed original characteristics of the principal known, historic language families, is that we have no reasonably precise date for the first appearance of what might be defined as a distinctly human species on this planet. One of the principal problems is, that for about 100,000 years or more of our past, a great part of the northern hemisphere of the planet lay under glacial ice, and the seas and oceans ranged between three and four hundred feet lower than during a recent period longer than 6,000 to 4,000 years, perhaps, as a reasonable rough estimate, as recently as a catrastrophic set of developments dating, according to Plato's sources, from about 13,000-12,000 years ago.

Given the evidence, that regularly recurring ice ages have dominated the northern continents of our planet for about two millions years, at least, we would expect to find most early traces of the human species in those areas which were not under glaciation, and in what were coastal regions at times when the oceans' levels were hundreds of feet lower than during our present interglacial warming period, a period of perhaps about 21,000 years to date. For similar reasons, sites at which we might expect to find ancient traces of the human species would include Africa and South America, and the region between the Tropics of Cancer and Capricorn generally.

There is one most important fact which aids us in sorting out some of the most relevant evidence. Suppose an archeologist discovers bones which he or she wishes to classify as either early man or a forerunner of our species. What is the difference between such residues, which might seem to resemble "early man," and a well-defined human specimen?

The answer is: We must focus upon the artifacts we uncover. We are searching for artifacts which reflect the presence of a human mind. Take the throwing spears dated from a site in Germany several hundred thousand years ago, for example.[9] Campfire sites associated with bones of animals, are an example. Similarly, we have in caves in France, examples of actually refined art, presently dated from tens of thousands of years prior to the melting of the last glaciation. The presense of such refined art, reflects a rather highly cultivated mind, which certainly had some form of written language 20,000-40,000 years ago.

Thus, we make a rule. When we say "human," rather than "ape," we should signify a species which shows the distinctive characteristic of human behavior: cognition, as I have defined cognition here. I mean to emphasize the distinction between learning, and transmission of learned behavior, which apes and others, such as dogs, can do, and a species which is capable of discovering and governing itself by validatable universal physical principles, or, in other words, ideas. Cognition, as I have defined it here, is the definition of man, and of specifically human behavior, including language.

Look at the cave paintings in France again. Cave sites are among the most important archeological sites for human finds—wherever human artifacts do occur. Such caves are among the likely places for either dwellings or burial sites. The evidence of language-behavior we seek in such sites, is of two types: art and symbolism. By art, we mean art as Classical Greek sculptors would tend to classify the artifact as art. The use of counting slashes associated with crude representations of animals, we would tend to view as a form, or approximation of a written language.

Granted, the evidence is sparse, but amid all of the uncertainties, certain kinds of conclusions can be, and must be adduced. More important than the few firm conclusions to be allowed, are the crucial questions which we can not put aside easily. All of those crucial questions arise when we examine the shards of ancient human existence, from the same standpoint we are obliged to apply to distinguish classroom behavior which represents mere learning, from classroom behavior which represents knowledge-in-the-making: cognition. Whatever must be said of ancient languages and proto-languages, all that is distinctly human, is that which pertains to the discovery of validatable forms of universal principles, of ideas as Plato defined ideas.

Thus, the ancient Sanskrit philologist Panini insisted, not nouns, but only verbs are real. Thus, when we hear speech in which the stress is habitually on the nouns, we are confronted with the use of language

---

9. Hartmut Thieme, "Lower Paleolithic Hunting Spears from Germany," *Nature*, Feb. 27, 1997, pp. 807-810; Robin Dennell, "The World's Oldest Spears," Feb. 27, 1997, pp. 767-768.

which is coincident with illiterate mental behavior. In literate mental behavior, we hear the emphasis usually placed upon the verb, or what we may distinguish as the "verbal action." The issue, once again, is "connecting the dots."

Nouns are "dots." Nominalist behavior, such as that of the English empiricists and the continental Enlightenment, presumes a deductive connection among the dots. The real connection, the functional relations which the dots express, are always in the non-linear form of verbal action, as Kepler and Gauss defined planetary orbits. Verbs pertain to the non-linear, e.g., non-deductive, mode of transformation associated with the characteristic form of action indicated by reference to a specific form of verbal action.

In other words, we must adopt a Riemannian view of the distinction between nominal forms of "dots," and characteristic forms of transformations within the manifold in respect to which the whole argument is made. Nouns are the domain of formalist mathematics; verbal action, especially transformations from a domain corresponding to one manifold, to a domain corresponding to a higher-order manifold, is the domain of change which corresponds to physical reality.

Compare literate speakers from earlier during this century, to speakers representing the succession of victims of post-war education and related enculturation. Look at the television set; listen to the radio. Hear everyday conversations. More and more, our population is losing the power of literate speech, is speaking an intrinsically illiterate kind of Orwellian run-on, which is fairly described as television-screen "teleprompterese," or, worse, "informationspeak."

In former, more literate—more intelligent—times, a knowing speaker spoke and wrote in ways which communicated literate ideas. The parts of his, or her paragraph were uttered, or punctuated, in ways which set the elements of composed statement ideas into their proper separation and relationship. All of this was uttered with emphasis upon the relevant verbal action. From his, or her statement, for example, one could write the corresponding formula, nicely sorted out, on the blackboard.

As Carl Zuckmayer described a demonstration by the actor Werner Krauss, a professional actor could conceal his face behind a Grecian mask, and make that mask itself appear to smile, or weep with sadness from the way the voice and movements from behind the mask imparted such notions to the audience. Those among us who learned something of the Classical poetry tradition, including Shakespeare, Keats, and Shelley in English, used what we learned from such great actors, to increase our ability to communicate ideas with a resulting improvement in the ability to impart far more profound and impassioned ideas than could be expressed in crude, illiterate street-corner speech. Now, the stage is silly, and the voices of the great actors are gone from that ruined place where the great actors fought, and lost their last great battles for the ability of audiences to impart and receive important ideas.

As Shelley said: we must seek a time and condition when there is an increase in the power of receiving and imparting profound and impassioned ideas respecting man and nature. That is what secondary education must do with the domain of poetry and song.

4.4 Poetry and Metaphor

The first step in secondary education in poetry, is to make clear that Aristotle's false definition of metaphor is to be rejected. Also, Thomas Hobbes' hateful view of metaphor, is not only to be excluded from the definitions of use of language. Against both Hobbes and Aristotle, the choice of Plato's use of metaphor is required, if competence is to be maintained in the classroom. For the relatively more gifted student, the presentation of Plato's *Parmenides* dialogue, as a powerful demonstration of the axiomatic folly of Aristotle's mis-definition of metaphor, as also the follies of the Eleatics and Sophists, is strongly recommended.

By metaphor, we must understand that that term signifies, in the general use of language, or in art, the same kind of conception as the posing of an ontological paradox within the domain of physical-science practice. A legitimate ontological paradox, or metaphor, is one which confronts the hearer with evidence which overthrows the assumption which the hearer may be presumed to bring to the subject matter of the poem, or other artistic composition being presented. The proof that this apparent contradiction in terms, is a valid one, forces the mind of the hearer to reconsider that, his or her view of the subject-matter within which the opening of the discussion was situated. Making this connection clear, is an essential task of secondary education in language and Classical art. A classroom discussion of the topics of William Empson's *Seven Types of*

EIRNS/Stuart Lewis

Bassoonist Mindy Pechenuk gives a demonstration of how her instrument can be made to "sing," like the human voice, at a conference of the Schiller Institute and International Caucus of Labor Committees on Sept. 5, 1999.

Ambiguity,[10] taken in light of my argument here, is a recommended feature of the curriculum. Examples from Shakespeare, Keats, and Shelley, and from the German Classical poetry of Goethe, Schiller, and Heine, are typical of appropriate topics of that discussion. English translations of the German Classical poetry should be designed to conform with underlining the specific metaphors and other ironies within the original German.

In other words, a metaphor is of the same nature, as to form, as the ontological paradox which obliges the thinker to discover a validatable new universal physical principle.

In a Classical poetic composition, or any analogous artistic composition, the composer uses a succession of ironies. For example, in simple strophic forms, each strophe may add an irony to an accumulation, such that the final metaphor is reached as a kind of crescendo of idea-ferment, toward which each preceding strophe has been leading, one after the other. Often, the recognition

---

10. William Empson, *Seven Types of Ambiguity* (Middlesex: Penguin Books, 1961).

of this function of the successive strophes must be supplied to the hearers by the singer of the poem, or Classical song; it is implied in the written composition, but, to be heard, it must be recognized by the singer in such a way that the audience hears it, and recognizes its validity, too.

In the German Classical song, as first defined by Wolfgang Mozart's famous *Das Veilchen* and *Abendempfindung*, and as typified by Beethoven, Schubert, Schumann, and Brahms later, there is a relatively unique refinement of poetic composition, which can, with some difficulties, and patience, be presented to English-speaking secondary pupils. A good secondary program will make clear why the Goethe who defended the composer Reichardt's relatively dull, but well-crafted settings of Goethe's poetry, was wrong, relative to Friedrich Schiller, on the issue of poetic musicality. Since Reichardt's compositions are available, a secondary teacher qualified in the German can present an English-language lecture and discussion of these issues, that in ways which are accessible to a non-German-speaking classroom.

On this issue, Goethe disapproved of Mozart's settings of Goethe poems, and Schubert and Beethoven supported Schiller's view of the matter against Goethe. Similarly, Heine and Schumann rejected the Romanticism into which Goethe was lured, during the period after Napoleon's victory over the Prussians at Jena-Auerstadt. The Classical musical setting of Classical poetry, in the mode introduced by Mozart's *Das Veilchen*, provides, unfortunately only within the bounds of German, a relatively unique insight to the musicality of Classical poetry in general. Shakespeare, Keats, and Shelley were better understood as poets by taking this implication of the German Classical song into account. That tactic for song-composition, affords the secondary student a more efficient insight, into not only all Classical poetry, but also effective modes of speech in general.

Look at such Classical song-settings in the light of C. Zuckmayer's reference to an incident with the actor Werner Krauss. The function of a Classical musical restatement of Classical poetry, is not to "set the poem to song." The object is to bring forth from the poem, something otherwise usually missed about the idea-content of the poem. In other words, the function of the Classical song-setting is to make the intended poetic utterance apparent to the hearer.

Again, the common error to be overcome, is the tendency of the miseducated novice to "connect the dots," to perform what passes for a "standard" recitation, and super-imposed interpretation, upon the poem, or the musical score: the tendency to sing the notes, instead of the music. One must utter Classical poetry (and song) as Furtwängler conducted: one must not recite the text, either from the written copy, or from memory of the written text as such. One must deliver a "recomposition" of the experience of the original composer's final version of his, or her original composition. This means that one must speak, and sing, not from mere memory of the "interpreted" text: one must unleash those cognitive processes which are reflected in the original composer's composition of the poem or song. The singer of the poem must become, for himself or herself, and for the hearers, the living cognitive process of composing that poem.

Recall my earlier reference to the cognitive experience of re-enacting an original discovery of a validatable universal physical principle. One must think, similarly, of re-creating the act of composing a poem, or song, not reciting a learned text upon which one has superimposed a stylized or otherwise contrived "interpretation." One should note that the great Classical conductors were usually trained *bel canto* singers, who utilized that voice-training as an integral part of their conducting. Also, such conductors did not merely know the entire composition they directed; they had often, as in the case of Furtwängler, re-enacted the process of the composer's original composing of the work. Thus, the performance flowed not from mere learning and superimposed interpretation of a memorized score, but was a reliving of the experience of the cognitive process of composition of the original work. Indeed, the best Classical musical performers were those who were driven to improve their cognitive reading of the works which dominated their performance repertoire, even several times over, even many years later.

The significance of this point is difficult to impart to the student, without some painstaking attention to what today's typical student (and younger adult) has usually lost: the recognition of the inherent musicality of literate forms of speaking of prose. This loss usually cripples speakers and hearers, alike, seriously, respecting their ability to communicate important classes of ideas through the spoken—and also the written—word. The issue is not whether the student appreciates poetry competently; the issue is whether the student's mind is cultivated, through poetry and music, to the degree that student's powers of speaking prose are developed to the level of rationality which the tasks of modern social life require.

Without a mastery of the Classical musical-poetical requirements of literate composition and hearing of speech in general, modern functional literacy in communication of important ideas, can not be achieved.

Too typically, the student in modern schools tends to understand poetic recitation as a kind of chiefly monotonous, but often inappropriately colored sing-song. What is needed, is a mastery of the notion of the use of Classical forms of poetry, and poetry's inherent musicality, to accomplish the transmission of impassioned important ideas even in speaking simple prose.

It might be useful to have an accounting report composed and read in a translation which serves as a caricature of today's commonly practiced—and awful!—poetic sing-song. This clinical demonstration could afford the pupils a memorable example of what poetry is properly intended to accomplish, to what purpose, and to make clear what subject-matters, such as ordinary accounting, are, by their nature, most ill-suited to poetry.

The general function of the pupil's obligatory mastery of Classical poetry and song, in secondary education, is not to produce either professional poets and singers, or professional critics of such works. The purpose of including this education as a standard requirement, is to cultivate better minds, minds more capable, as Shelley wrote, of "imparting and receiving profound and impassioned conceptions respecting man and nature."

Passion? This brings us to the matter of coloration in speech. It is sufficient, for our purposes here, to point out certain among the more basic devices of coloration available in vocal and instrumental composition and performance. I limit myself to those aspects of musical, and musical-like coloration, which are indispensable for poetry, and also required for literate speaking (and writing) of prose.

There is tempo. In musical notation, we have various forms of "Allegro," as "Allegretto," "Andante," "Adagio," or "Largo." Contrary to devotees of the metronome (which Beethoven, for example, was not), these notations do not signify stop-watch speeds; in Classical tradition, they correspond to a mood, or, "modality." These notions of tempi are properly applicable, as forcefully, to spoken prose, as to formal musical performances. They represent a way of coloring an utterance to impart a state of mind.

Among the better, matured professional musicians, the work of serious composers is never addressed with a specific metronomic reading in mind.[11] The secondary student should re-enact the discovery of the principle governing choice of tempo, in speaking prose, respecting the quality of idea-material being presented at that stage of an argument. The student should then consider the relevance of that to the tempo (and use of rubato and caesura, e.g., written commas) in oral presentation of poems.

There are six possible, trainable but natural, general types of singing voice, and of speaking voice. These are defined by the Florentine style of *bel canto* voice-training, each defined in terms of what is called "register shift" ("voice registration"). These types are multiplied by different qualities of voices of the same registral types.[12]

There are different qualities of voice-coloration defined by vocalization (e.g., darker versus lighter vowels). There are the effects of consonant-vowel combinations on coloration.

There are also superimposed other modes of voice-coloration, which might lighten a darker vocalization, or darken a lighter one, as the music requires this.

These matters of registration, various types within each registral type, vocalization, and other coloration, are built-in features of the composition of Classical polyphony. Indeed these are virtually the definition of the basis for Classical polyphony. These are also essential features of the singing of poetry, or of speaking in prose modes, as by the best Classical actors.

By use of this repertoire of means available, the poet, or speaker of a poem, or prose, is enabled to color utterance both to indicate the voice of different speakers, and to indicate a shift in mood within the mind of any among those speakers, including the poet's own autobiographical voice.

The secondary student will better understand such matters, when he, or she is freed from the unfortunately popular delusion, that "instrumental music" is to be differentiated from singing, within the domain of Classical composition.

In addressing the problems posed to the orchestra,

EIRNS/Stuart Lewis

The late Eliane Magnan, one of the great 'cellists of the Twentieth Century, and a friend of LaRouche and the Schiller Institute. "A change in fingering," LaRouche writes, "may be the means by which the violinist, violist, or 'cellist 'sings' in one human singing-voice registration, or another. Or, the mastery of bowing permits the musician to effect a register-shift through a change in coloration."

the conductor has two alternatives. One, a popular one, is to homogenize the "orchestral voice." The other, which often meets strong resistance among today's instrumentalists, is to recognize that the instruments of the Classical orchestral palette were developed as imitations of the human singing voice.

The accomplished professional wind instrumentalist does not "blow" into the instrument, but, more emphatically, sings into it, as all the best oboists, for example, do. With the string instruments, a shift from one string to another, has the effect of a register-shift. Thus, a change in fingering may be the means by which the violinist, violist, or 'cellist "sings" in one human singing-voice registration, or another. Or, the mastery of bowing permits the musician to effect a register-shift through a change in coloration.

In well-tempered counterpoint, where the disso-

---

11. For example, the metronome readings for the first and last movements of Beethoven's keyboard sonata, Opus 106, are wrong. With Beethoven, for example, one never performs fugues "too fast."
12. *A Manual on the Rudiments of Tuning and Registration,* op cit.

nance generated from inversions is key to the developmental process of the composition, vox-humana-like voice-registration is indispensable. If homogenization is superimposed, the awkwardness of a purely instrumental approach to performance may be obscured, but the idea-content of the counterpoint is lost. In major choral works with orchestra, failure to treat the orchestra as a chorus subject to human singing-voice definitions of registration, may produce either ugly effects, or fake the ensemble's way through the composition, through a dehumanizing homogenization.

If voice-registration and coloration are respected throughout, the quality of the final outcome will lie in the approach the conductor and performers take, toward bringing out the developmental continuity of the work performed. What are otherwise either sausage-string-style discontinuities, or ugly dissonances, vanish, as dissonance of various sorts dissolves into developmental transitions—as a proper performance of the fugue from either Beethoven's Opus 106 or Opus 110, typifies the case.

The purpose and meaning of the presentation of music, so composed and performed, to a lay musical audience, such as average secondary pupils, should be made clear in the educational program. This clarity is to be achieved, by leading the pupils to the recognition, that the social function of mastering Classical poetry and Classical musical composition, in these respects, is to cultivate the ability of all of the pupils to speak and write intelligently, through application of these features of musicality to prose utterances, as the best Classical actors have done. The mastering of speaking, writing, reading, and hearing prose from this poetical-musical vantage-point, is the quality of communication indispensable to the cultivated mind of every citizen.

4.5 Passion and Thinking

Listen to the Orwellian "teleprompterese" and "informationspeak," which pollutes the traffic in both mass-media and private intercourse today. Be reminded of other marvelous novelties of our times, such as a so-called university education lately liberated from study of the works of "dead, white, European males (DWEMs)." Such are the marvelous novelties which have been lately dropped from the tree of "value-free education."

The Orwellian newscast's interviewer speaking "informationspeak": "How did you feel about watching the slaughter of your children, Mrs. Jones?," is, like the executioner "Just doing my job," a true example of "value-free" behavior. Like the worst kind of Federal bureaucrat, no mass-murderer is so criminal as the one who plies his cruel profession with the cold logic of "I can feel your pain, ma'am; but, I'm just doing my job."

In the way some people, like TV newscasters, utter Orwellese today, we experience the sheer bestiality of those who have been educated to speak and act like "Third Wave" robots, trained to speak and act without a flicker of conscience. Only in reply to a sensed affront to the bureaucratic machine which has programmed their behavior, do they exhibit what passes, among them, for expressions of sincere indignation. They have been programmed, not to think, but only to calculate according to currently approved statistical, sociologists' formulas. "I'm just connecting the dots, ma'am. Nothing personal."

The trouble is, that as the mass media has assumed the trappings of an Orwellian god, foolish little people find a sense of self-importance, in feigning styles which imitate, like suggestible children, the "teleprompterese" and "informationspeak" of those media celebrities whom they regard as the authorities who are to be imitated.

Such types do show passion, at times. Like the fabled "Lord of the Flies," today's value-free veterans of the 1960s campuses, often find a substitute for honest passion, in showing homicidal indignation when someone breaks their currently concocted rules for winning the game, such as those current fads of "cutting the social welfare budget," which their crowd just made up. They are very angry at times, even sadistically cruel, but never moral, always value-free. It is not a matter of morals; like a lunatic desire to become an "alpha dog," it is their transiently current "thing."

Until these Orwellian times, since Plato's best-known writing, known as *The Republic*, civilized representatives of European civilization had located morality in a commitment to truthfulness and justice.

The notable exceptions to morality have included the ancient pagan Romans, and the modern empiricists, Kantians, positivists, and existentialists. All these, like Immanuel Kant and his existentialist followers, have defended their errant beliefs and policies on the presumption that truth, and therefore justice, are unknowable; they find a substitute for truth in what they currently consider, collectively, to be convenient for their own purpose. For them, justice is delimited to the more or less arbitrary decisions of law and other traditions, which their crowd, such as the Wall Street crowd of bankers and lawyers, just made up.

That latter view was the dogma of England's Thomas Hobbes, John Locke, Bernard Mandeville, Adam Smith, and Jeremy Bentham. It is the current, radical-positivist, and often frankly racist wave of judicial policy-shaping, under the Rehnquist U.S. Supreme Court. It is through the latter trend in U.S., as in British notions of so-called "rule of law," that our own and other nations have been gripped, increasingly, by the Orwellian nightmare of "teleprompterese" and "informationspeak."

A Passion for Truth

Put aside the formalist's cult of putatively unimpassioned deduction; where does passion lie in Classical art, and what values does that passion express? The answer to such questions lies, axiomatically, within the domain of cognition.

The essential passion of civilized life, is that zeal for truth and justice which Plato associates with the Greek term *agapē*. This is the same quality of passion which the Christian Apostle Paul underlines so famously in Chapter 13 of his First Letter to the Corinthians, the Chapter from which Johannes Brahms excerpts the text for the fourth of his *Four Serious Songs*.

This is the same passion we experience summoned within us, when we muster a stubborn, effective form of cognitive exertion, for discovering a cognitive solution for the type of ontological paradoxes which are characteristic of the discovery of validatable universal physical or artistic principles. Such is the passion of cognitive action; such is the verbal action which transforms our axiomatic world-outlook, our so-called mind-set, from a relatively inferior to a superior condition.

The cultivated mind, or, if you prefer, the civilized individual mind, reacts with the greatest mustering of passion, to issues of what it believes to be validated universal principle, principles of Classical art as much as universal physical principles. These principles serve as the axioms of our decision-making. The defense of such a principle, or, in the alternative, its necessary su-

percession by a higher principle, is the location of the noblest mustering of passion respecting what may be termed moral issues. Here, as nowhere else, lie the life and death issues of civilization itself. Here lies the central task and purpose of public education. Here lies that passion which is the motive power of both scientific discovery and valid Classical-artistic composition. Here lies the passion of that moral faculty which sets actually moral persons in opposition to the like of empiricists, Kantians, positivists, and existentialists. This passion is the substance of ideas.

This connection is shown most dramatically in terms of the functions of irony and especially metaphor, in all Classical art. It is precisely that quality of passion, which sets true Classical art, and morality generally, apart from what passes generally for both entertainment and education today. The person who speaks Orwellian "teleprompterese" or "informationspeak," is to be seen as symptomatic of a profound, essentially sado-masochistic—e.g., "bi-polar," moral degeneration permeating both the educational systems and other dominant features of so-called mass culture today. In such affected, intrinsically inhuman, currently popularized, styles of speaking, there is the stench of violence, which the speaker has done to his, or her mind, a brutish wont for imitative conformity to one's masters, like those victims of Nazi concentration-camps, who sought to restyle their prison garb in likeness to the uniforms of their captors.

As one of history's greatest tragedians and historians, Friedrich Schiller, put the point: the function of the Classical tragedy is to bring audiences from the theater better people than they had entered it. Such is Shakespeare's use of the history of Richard III; such is Hamlet; such is Schiller's history-based account of the principle of the self-destruction of the true-life Philip II's Spain, in *Don Carlos*. In each case, the power of the stage has been used, to evoke from the members of the audience a sense of the tragic folly lurking generally in themselves, while also showing that audience its power to seize effective alternatives to such pathetic outcomes. This brings joy and optimism. It does so, by calling up the cognitive powers within the member of the audience, the power to resolve that ontological paradox from history, which the greatest artists present as tragedy, on stage.

On the same account, the poet Shelley pointed out the role of poets as the true legislators of mankind. It is the lessons of principles of the human mind, which are conveyed by the medium of Classical artistic composition, which elevate a people's capacity to muster those forms of cooperative relations, by means of which the real-life problems of life are mastered in a cooperative way. So, the masterful development of polyphony by Bach, and by such followers as Mozart, exemplifies the way in which great Classical art brings people together joyfully—in passion—to cultivate those habits of mind, by means of which daily life and moments of crisis are set upon upward paths.

Underlying all that, there is the passion called *agapē*, the passion, the emotional impetus, which is the natural verbal action of cognition.

The difference between the deductive formalist and the Platonist, was always the difference between the corpse and the living, the difference between the death-like symbolism of Archaic art, and the sense of life in mid-motion, conveyed by great Classical sculpture and painting, the difference between a dead man composing, the notorious Rameau, and the vibrant breath of life permeating the compositions of a Bach and Mozart. Deductive argument is like death walking. It is the action manifest as a directed principle of change, as Plato's argument typifies the meaning of change, which distinguishes the human being from the beast,

It is that mental activity, through which validatable discoveries of universal principle are generated, through which man's power in and over the universe is increased, which, alone, represents knowing. It is the passion which underlies and permeates those transitions, permeates change in that sense, which is the essence of all Classical artistic and scientific knowledge. Deduction, by contrast, is nothing better than a corpse walking.

This brings us to the role of a science of physical economy, as the higher vantage-point from which to know the deeper purpose and underlying method required for the needed reform of U.S. secondary and higher education today.

5.0 Art and Economy

Among the nobler cleansing actions awaiting today's secondary and higher education institutions, is the eradication of the fraud of teaching bookkeeping under the misleading label of "economics." Ask yourself: "Do you know why that must be recognized, and widely, publicly condemned, as a fraud?" Considering the importance of economy in the life of virtually every household, knowing why that kind of teaching is a fraud, ought to be considered as about as essential a qualification for citizens reaching voting age, as the elements of personal and public hygiene. There are also other, urgent reasons for denouncing it publicly and widely wherever policies of education are under discussion.

However, the importance of nothing less than bare literacy in economics among graduates of secondary education, is merely one among the important reasons the issue of the cited fraud must be raised here. As I shall now show you, now, this goes far beyond the daily work of managing a family household's financial affairs, or managing a business enterprise.

Unfortunately, what has been usually taught, lately, under the heading of "economics" in most secondary and higher education, during the past fifty-odd years, is not even honest bookkeeping.[13] Most among today's professors of economics, claim, with aid of computer technology, to account for almost everything, excepting the sometimes terrible consequences for our nation, and the world, of their own militant ignorance of how economies actually work over a period as long as a generation or more.

The actual cause-and-effect for the crucial trends in real economies, does not lie within the domain of those kinds of "connect-the-dots" statistics, which simply compare the price-tags attached to (usually) countable objects. The real causes for increases and decreases of the physical productivity of national and world economy, per capita and per square kilometer of the Earth's surface-area, lie in the domain of physics, not bare-bottomed mathematics as such.

The real causes involve studying the way in which the discovery and application of new physical principles predetermines the potential level of productivity in economies. It requires study of the ways in which such scientific progress, based on fundamental scientific research, is variously used, neglected, or misused. Just as we measure the orbits of planets in compound

---

13. Typical is the way in which the U.S. government, fraudulently, added $249 billions of additional GDP for 1998, out of nothing but a bookkeeping trick which would have been considered fraudulent among old-fashioned, competent CPAs (see "It's Time to Dump GDP as a Measure of the Economy," *EIR*, Dec 10, 1999).

cycles, each of up to 100,000, or more years, the physical-economic effects of chosen investment policies, must be measured over the span of a half, single, or several generations. For purposes of planning for the effects of investment and related policies, and also education policies, a dozen to twenty-five years or so ahead, is a minimal period. The time from birth to maturity of each generation, is the minimal base-line for competent investment forecasting, and related policies. Looking at the effects of investment, or non-investment, in scientific progress three generations ahead, is the general basis for competent long-range policy-decisions of modern economies considered in their entirety.

This does not mean that economics consists of forecasting what might probably happen a generation or so from now. Competent economics defines the actions which must be taken, beginning now, to prevent undesired results a decade, or one or more generations ahead. What you fail to do this year, will cause the unpleasantness you will have caused by today's negligence, as much as a decade, a generation, or more later. In agriculture and manufacturing of modern products, the results of today's investments or negligence show up over a period of cycles as long as a dozen years to a generation. The effects of failing to make today's needed public improvements in basic economic infrastructure, may come back to haunt you for as long as two generations yet to come.

The long-term trends in real economy, of a generation or more, can be adequately understood, only by understanding what is meant by what the greatest modern mathematical physicists, such as Gauss and Riemann, defined as *a characteristic physical-space-time curvature*. To understand how technology shapes the future of the real economy, the Gauss-Riemann notion of such curvature must be applied to study of economies as physical-economic processes. The physics standard for understanding such long-term trends, is therefore what is properly termed *the Riemannian curvature* of physical-economic processes. It is that "curvature," and changes in that "curvature," which actually generates the observed pattern of observable "dots."[14] This use of the term "curvature," corresponds to the Kepler-Gauss definition of planetary orbits, as Gauss showed this for both geodesy and for the special case of the Keplerian orbits of the principal asteroids, and also for the case of the general principles of the curvature of physical space-time. If that connection is not competently understood, then no scientifically competent judgment of a modern nation's long-range economic, and educational policies, can be provided.

Neither the teacher, student, nor layman should be frightened by what may seem, to many, to be unfamiliar terminology. Economics is, predominantly, a branch of physical science, which can be mastered, on various levels, as any other science can be mastered in secondary and higher education. One requires nothing but the appropriate education and related experience, to make the subject-matter clear in a practical way. Happily, the rudiments of such competence are within the reach of any competent secondary education program for today.

So, today's commonplace misunderstanding of how economies work, presents us, once again, with the same issue, of the nouns versus the verbs, which confronts the student in the classroom's science and Classical art.

For example, the famous Keynesian Professor Joan Robinson, of England's Cambridge University, spoke fairly when she described today's still-popular quack economist, Professor Milton Friedman, as a devotee of "*post hoc, ergo propter hoc*" superstitions.[15] Now, as then, Friedman's continued appeal to his dupes, has been that he fit his ignorance to suit the prejudices and fantasies of greedy and simple-minded, so-called "mainstream opinion." The intrinsic absurdity of Friedman's teaching, is his adoption of the fallacy of substituting mere nouns for verbs: his use of arbitrary linear statistical methods, instead of accounting for the prin-

---

14. In former times, twenty years and more ago, competent production management in the U.S.A., Germany, Japan, and so on, based its practice in the design of both products and productive processes, on the same kind of thinking and practice which the designer of machine-tools used: the methods of experimental physics, as applied to designs and testing of products and processes. The mathematical doctrine which applies to such competent production-management practice, is to be found in the principles of Bernhard Riemann's *Über die Hypothesen, welche der Geometrie zu Grunde liegen* (1854): in *Bernhard Riemanns Gesammelte mathematische Werke* H. Weber, ed., (New York: Dover Publications reprint, 1953). The LaRouche-Riemann Method in economic analysis, is based upon the addition of Riemann's discovery to solve a problem which had been posed by an original economics discovery by me.

15. Joan Robinson, *Economic Heresies* (New York: Basic Books, 1971).

cipled character of the processes which transform choices of expenditures and investments, into measurable changes in the physical-economic productivity of the economy as a whole.

Moving from the relatively simple-minded chatter of Professor Friedman and his devotees, to the "ivory tower" world of today's wild-eyed Wall Street gambler, the "mathematical economics" of John von Neumann's followers, only carries the commonplace ignorance of a Professor Friedman, to the outer limits of linear fantasy-life. Very little more than a handful of mathematical complications has been added to today's so-called "mathematical economics," since von Neumann proposed publicly, about 1938, that every economic process could be reduced to a matter of solutions for simultaneous linear inequalities.

As the August-September 1998 crash of Wall Street's Long Term Capital Management (LTCM) attests, the way in which LTCM's Nobel Prize-winning Black-Scholes formula nearly sank the Wall Street system,[16] shows that von Neumann's techniques differ chiefly from Friedman's, in that von Neumann's influence has the power to create bigger financial cataclysms than Friedman had ever dreamed. Experiences such as the LTCM scandal are also to be seen as a condemnation of those, such as Federal Reserve Chairman Alan Greenspan, who have insisted in practice, that, in such matters, exuberantly bigger is necessarily better.

The question here, is not of the type usually discussed in today's classroom and textbook. Economics comes into design of educational policy, as it does here, when we ask the question: How might we measure the performance of different policies proposed for secondary and higher education? On this point, we are not limiting the economic effects of educational policy to the effects of education in economics itself. I mean the economic impact of the whole of secondary (and also higher) education, including education in physical science, Classical artistic composition, and history, on the

---

16. In 1997, the Royal Swedish Academy of Sciences awarded the Nobel Prize for Economics to Robert Merton and Myron Scholes for developing "a pioneering formula for the valuation of stock options." Their work, the Academy stated, "generated new types of financial instruments and facilitated more efficient risk management in society." At the time, Merton and Scholes were partners in Long-Term Capital Management, which placed trillions of dollars in derivatives bets based upon their prize-winning formulae. In September 1998, LTCM failed spectacularly, forcing the Federal Reserve to orchestrate a bailout of the firm to keep the global derivatives market from collapsing, and taking the entire global financial and monetary system with it.

future physical-economic productivity of the entire labor-force.

In other words, how do different choices of educational policies effect desired, or undesired changes in the future physical-economy productivity of the average graduate? If we examine the functional relationship between Classical-artistic development and economy, the notion of education's performance as a relatively measurable magnitude, becomes clearer than could be shown in any different way. This means defining the subject of economics in a different way than has been generally done in schools and universities of recent times.

The currently ongoing, 1991-1999, terminal phase of the thirty-year downturn of the world's present financial and monetary system, is to be seen as the result of a systemic incompetence in the policy-making of leading governments, that over that period of about thirty years or longer. The presently escalating world financial crisis, if looked at from the standpoint of comparing physical market-baskets, rather than simply money prices, shows that the economies of Europe and the Americas (in particular), have been in general decline throughout those recent thirty years, most clearly since August 1971.

This decline has been the result of increasingly defective economic and related policies of both governments and supranational institutions. However, the true cause for the pattern of decline, taken as a whole, lies in those post-1966 shifts in cultural outlooks, including changes in the cultural standpoint of secondary and other educational policies, which have caused the population to prefer those trends in successive changes in economic policies, which latter have had the relatively worst effect on these nations and the world at large.

The fact that the most powerful combination of the world's governments, has tolerated the folly of such a failed set of policies, for so many decades of erosion in the physical economy of their nations, reflects a Classically tragic quality of cultivated ignorance among that majority of the citizens, which has either elected, or simply tolerated the political authorities responsible for those trends in policy-shaping.

There is that to be considered, but also much more: much deeper issues of education in general are involved. In fact, as I shall show now, it is no exaggeration to say, that a competent understanding of real economy, is the point of reference from which to judge what education as a whole must be. The student could never begin to understand either real economy, or the related standards for adjudging the relative success of educational policies, until certain corresponding highlights of ancient and modern history were made clear.

Economics as History

If one means by "economics," the study of the means by which mankind's per-capita power in and over the universe is improved, then, the evidence of the currently accelerating world-wide financial crisis shows, that most of the medicine currently purveyed as academic economics, as at MIT or Harvard Business School, for example, is the disease most urgently to be eradicated.

As I have already stated here, contrary to most such academics, economics is essentially a branch of physical science. This science emerged during and following the Fifteenth-Century, so-called "Golden," Renaissance. There is no mere coincidence in the fact, that this was the same Renaissance which gave birth to the founding of modern experimental physical science, by Cardinal Nicholas of Cusa and his collaborators and followers of the middle through late Fifteenth Century. Leonardo da Vinci was among the most outstanding of such students of Cusa's founding of modern physical science. Born at Florence, economics took on the attributes of national economy, first in Louis XI's France, and then in Henry VII's England.

At that time, this practice of political economy represented a body of practice intricately linked with the revolutionary upsurge of a new kind of institution in Europe, the modern, sovereign nation-state. In principle, this new kind of state had nothing in common with the laws, or the conception of the human individual in ancient Babylon, the Roman Empire, or with feudalism. The new kind of state represented the notion of government as based entirely upon that same principle, of the general welfare, which was later set forth in our 1776 Declaration of Independence and the Preamble of our 1789 Federal Constitution.

These Renaissance novelties of statecraft were associated then, and thereafter, with the greatest rate of improvement in the physical and other conditions of life among affected populations. Until the recent downturn in the economy of Europe and the Americas, since 1971-1972, the model of the modern, sovereign nation-state economy, sparked the greatest rate of demographic and related progress in all known human existence up to that time. No known form of society has been able even to approach the level of improvement of the human condition, which has been accomplished under the umbrella of that modern sovereign nation-state which was born in Europe during the Fifteenth Century.

Our United States was created as a nation founded upon those constitutional principles, created so at a time when the old feudal traditions prevented that form of republic from being consolidated in any part of old Europe. With all of our failings, and despite the nests of evil in powerful positions within our nation, we were, in our best times, the best of all republics.

The developments in Europe, from the Council of Florence through Louis XI's France, Henry VII's England, and Isabella I's backing of Christopher Columbus' use of Toscanelli's maps, by aid of which he rediscovered the Americas, brought about a profound, but always imperilled revolution in the nature of government and of the notions of public law. Prior to these Renaissance, revolutionary changes in law and general practice, the prevailing feudal notions of law and of statecraft, were rooted in the doctrine of imperial law, the imperial tradition of "world government," of Babylon, ancient Rome, and feudalism. The Venice-directed Welf League's launching of its ruinous wars against the Emperor Frederick II, which resulted in the Fourteenth Century's "New Dark Age," are typical of both the Roman imperial tradition and of Romantic feudalism. That wicked set of old ideas of "world government," is today the new, wild-eyed utopianism, by means of which the present-day enemies of the sovereign nation-state are determined to degrade human existence, throughout our planet, that as quickly as possible.

In broad terms, all of today's competent teaching and practice of economics, is consistent, in fundamentals, with Gottfried Leibniz's standard set for national physical economy, as set by economists such as U.S. Treasury Secretary Alexander Hamilton, and such followers of Hamilton as Mathew and Henry Carey, and Germany's Friedrich List.

The opponents of that American System, those who teach bookkeeping in the name of "economics," represent a tradition copied from the British East India Company's Haileybury School tradition. That British tradition, in turn, was chiefly a copy of schemes drawn up by earlier, Venetian advocates of merciless population control. These latter included such predecessors of Haileybury's Rev. Thomas Malthus, as Giovanni Botero and Giammaria Ortes. Hence, among English-speaking ideologues, the tendency to adopt policies which promote genocide, or related crimes against humanity, is typified by the work of Bernard Mandeville, by Jeremy Bentham's fellow-ideologues of the Haileybury School, and the modern followers of Mandeville, the Mont Pelerin Society, which gave the world the kinds of disasters, at Paddington railway station and elsewhere, propagated by Mont Pelerin's screeching U.K. Prime Minister, Margaret Thatcher.

Under the pre-Renaissance tradition of Babylon, pagan Rome, and European feudalism, the state was the personal property of an emperor, or of an oligarchy controlling the functions of a Mesopotamian or Roman emperor. This arrangement was known generically, notably since the time of Aristotle's teacher, Isocrates, as "the oligarchical model." The state, as it existed under that model, was implicitly the personal property of that government, and law itself was defined by a notion of "reason of state," consistent with the same oligarchical model famously enshrined in the brutish Magna Carta.

The people ruled over by that oligarchy, were either simply the slaves of, or otherwise treated as the human cattle, as subjects of the property-title represented by that form of state. Nearly fifteen centuries must pass, from the time of the Roman Emperors Augustus, Tiberius, and Nero, until the first approximation of a modern form of sovereign state—President Abraham Lincoln's government of, by, and for its people, would emerge, in the aftermath of the Fifteenth-Century Council of Florence.

Thus, the first attempt to regulate the performance of the state according to the continuing improvement of the condition of all of the people, had to wait until the emergence of the first approximations of the modern nation-state, that of France under Louis XI, and the establishment of Louis XI's model in England, under Henry VII. That Renaissance change from such precursors of modern nation-state economy, as those predecessors established under Charlemagne, the influence of Peter Abelard, and the Hohenstaufen Emperor Frederick II, was the birth of the teaching of a scientific form of economics.

The significance of the Fifteenth-Century change in the definition of the state, is clearer, if we look at the trend of the recent thirty-odd years, a trend toward a return to the kind of imperialism, sometimes called "world government," or "globalization." "Globalization" today, is essentially an attempted revival of the old imperial system which had once dominated European political, legal, and social institutions, under the Roman Empire and medieval feudalism. Typical of that recent trend, are the assigning of an axiomatic value to "free trade" as such, and the spread of an even more wicked, radically Lockean version of the same dogma, "shareholder value." The essential, axiomatic difference between the American System and the British monarchy's "free trade" system, lies in the American System's notion of "general welfare," or what emergent modern nation-state civilization indicated by the use of the English term "commonwealth."

The old, pre-Fifteenth-Century political model, under the Babylonian, Roman, and medieval systems, was the same model so crudely and shamelessly professed, later, by fanatical defenders of the Confederacy and its system of African-American chattel slavery. Those moral degenerates who apologized for the Confederacy's system of slavery as "a peculiar institution," insisted that slavery had enabled "The South" to produce a class of (self-esteemed) "genteel" parasites, the latter esteemed, by these parasites, as of a nobler culture than Yankee industrialists and other louts.[17] That is typical of the Roman imperial tradition, the Babylonian-Roman tradition of the state as the property of a ruling class of oligarchical "shareholders," and the subjects of that state, as Vice-President Al Gore's *Earth in the Balance* argued, as virtually classes of expendable "human cattle," "human cattle" to be nourished, fattened, milked, and slaughtered at the pleasure of the gentry which owned them. Such is today's revival of the Nazi-like doctrine, that human beings are just other animals, with the same rights, and lack of human rights, as beasts of the farm, forest, and brushlands.

The same perverted viewpoint of the old Confederacy was continued, with a certain slyness, by fanatical "post-bellum" Anglophiles of the "Nashville Agrarian" type, such as Robert Penn Warren and Harvard Professor William Yandell Elliot. All of these sundry expressions of oligarchism, saw the only meaning for even the very existence of the victims of oligarchical rule, to lie within the sundry classes of services and amusement which a suitably obedient class of stupefied "human

---

17. The 1993 Nobel Economics Prize winners Robert Fogel and Douglass North shamelessly advocated slavery as an economic model. Fogel co-authored (with Stanley Engerman) *Time on the Cross: The Economics of American Negro Slavery*, which claimed that the plantation-slavery model was superior to the family farm. Gary Becker, the winner of the 1992 Economics Prize, has publicly called for setting up a market to trade in body parts, to allow those who can afford it to buy organs for transplant.

cattle"—a virtual class of rutting, babbling "Yahoos," as Jonathan Swift used that term—provided a ruling, aristocratic, class or race.

As any secondary-school graduate should know real-life history, for the Roman and feudal systems, as for the evil system of Babylon, earlier, the subject classes and "races" were viewed as justifying their existence only to the degree this suited the convenience, and the whims of the ruling oligarchy. The same oligarchical view of the populations of Africa, South America, and Asia, has been lately expressed by the Club of Rome, in Vice-President Al Gore's *Earth in the Balance*,[18] as Professor Elliot's former protégé, National Security Advisor Henry A. Kissinger's 1974 *National Security Study Memorandum 200*,[19] and the outgoing Carter Administration's *Global 2000*[20] and *Global Future*[21] expressed the same Malthusian doctrine.

As long as the imperial Code of Diocletian cast its brutish shadow legacy on both the Roman Empire in the east, and the feudalism of western Europe, there was no basis in government for the idea of measuring the performance of government, by the conditions government established for the benefit of the entire population and its posterity. If the oligarch was challenged to address the conditions of life and development of the people in general, his Christian conscience, such as he might have professed it to be, turned away from the conditions of the living, to slavemasters' unctuous references to "rewards to be harvested by the slaves in the next life."

The modern nation-state, and the very idea of a modern national economy, rests entirely upon the idea that the legitimate authority of government, is limited to that government's efficient concern for the general welfare and improvement of all of the people, and all of the land-area, and that for both the living and their posterity. That is the principle upon which the United States was founded, as the 1776 Declaration of Independence

---

18. Al Gore, Jr., *Earth in the Balance: Ecology and the Human Spirit* (New York: Houghton Mifflin, 1992).
1919 "National Security Study Memorandum 200: Implications of Worldwide Population Growth for U.S. Security and Overseas Interests," Dec. 10, 1994. For excerpts, see *EIR*, June 9, 1995, p. 18.
20. The White House Council on Environmental Quality (CEQ) and the U.S. State Department, *Global 2000 Report to the President,* 1980. For an analysis and excerpts, see "The Haig-Kissinger Depopulation Policy," *EIR*, March 10, 1981.
21. The White House Council on Environmental Quality (CEQ) and the U.S. State Department, *Global Future,* 1980.

defines the natural right of the U.S.A. to that independence. For the Babylonian, Roman, and feudal oligarchy, as for the monarchy of Britain's George III, as for Prince Metternich, the republican notion associated with the then recently established U.S. republic, was an idea to be crushed at birth.

Such was the crux of the political revolution finally unleashed by Europe's Fifteenth-Century Golden Renaissance. The growth of population and improvement of productivity and demographic characteristics of populations since, attests to the emergence of rates of improvement of the general welfare of the peoples of modern nation-states, of a degree never found earlier in any part of history or other evidence. Indeed, until very recent decades, the great yearning of the peoples of South America, Africa, and Asia generally, was to secure the right to conduct their affairs, as sovereign peoples, to the same demographic advantage seen in the best periods of history of modern Europe and the U.S.A.

Thus, modern economy, from its birth in the Fifteenth-Century emergence of the modern form of sovereign nation-state, produced a form of society committed to the principle of continuing progress in mankind's power in and over the universe, and of corresponding improvements in the condition of human life generally. The function of modern economy, was not to measure the rate of profit of individual enterprises, nor of the mere collection of such enterprises, but to adopt policies which ensured those forms of increase of the physical productive powers of labor, and related fertility of land-area, which would result in those improvements in the general welfare—for all of the population and all its posterity—which could be estimated and measured in terms of relevant effects.

Granted, that goals consistent with such effects are found, in germ, within parts of the history of the culture of ancient Greece. Granted, that Christianity was committed, from the beginning, to the universality of the human individual, not merely one language group, or religious party. To get out of the dark age which had benighted the Mediterranean region, since the rise of the power of pagan Rome, required a struggle of nearly fifteen centuries, until the first approximation of the modern sovereign nation-state, in the monarchies of France's Louis XI and England's Henry VII.

Thus, not only was the Fifteenth-Century Renaissance the beginning of the practice of new, pro-Christian standards of law and government in Europe, but it would not have been possible for modern economy to come into existence, without the introduction of a new form of government. The new form of government, as every literate, decently educated U.S. patriot knows, is the modern, sovereign nation-state republic, a republic whose nature is typified by President Abraham Lincoln's view of its governing principle and mission. Without the Fifteenth-Century Renaissance, that form, modern political-economy, would never have come into being.

Even the opposing modern systems of so-called "political economy," were not concocted until after the establishment of the first modern nation-states. This opposition came entirely from the far-flung financier oligarchy of Sixteenth- and Seventeenth-Century Venice. It was these Venetians, the same financial predators who had orchestrated the hundred years of warfare leading into what became known as the Fourteenth-Century European "New Dark Age," who created what became known as the Eighteenth-Century British model of political-economy. Their method in science, politics, and morals, that of Galileo and his student Thomas Hobbes, John Locke, Bernard Mandeville, Adam Smith, and Jeremy Bentham, simply "connected the dots." Their system interpreted everything in political economy from the same standpoint of the system of double-entry bookkeeping which had been invented by the most notorious of such Venetian assets as the notorious "Lombard" banking house of Bardi.

As the economic dogmas of Mandeville, France's Dr. François Quesnay, and Adam Smith show, these empiricists never considered any active physical principle as the cause of the pattern of behavior of their "dots"; each and all of these wildly superstitious, oligarchical lackeys—these virtual "Leporellos," assumed that there existed some magical principle, which caused the dots themselves to interact mechanically, and always to such an effect, to bring about the best result through a very large number of unfathomably mysterious, but purely mechanical interactions among these dots themselves.

That, as every one among today's rare, competently educated secondary school graduates knows, is the history of the birth of the controversy between what became known as the American System of political-economy, and its leading enemy, the British "free trade" model which Professor Milton Friedman, Friedrich von Hayek, and John von Neumann, each and all reduced to the absurdity of random mechanical interactions among mere "dots in themselves."

5.1 Physical Economy: Man and Nature

As every qualified graduate of a competent secondary education would know, the earliest known traces of scientific thinking began, with society's observation of the apparent regularity of the movements of the stars. The earliest known forms of the Zodiac, are simply that. From pre-historic times, we have evidence of calendars based on the calculations of regular cycles of change in the relationship of a point on the Earth, to the Zodiac, over not only the period of an equinoctial cycle, but the orbitally determined, regular ice-age cycles of as long as approximately 100,000 years.[22] This appeared in forms of combined astronomical calendars, and related systems of transoceanic navigation dated from long before historic times.

These calendars and related navigational systems avoided the error of assuming that there existed some direct, mechanical sort of "action at a distance" relationship among the "dots" in the sky. The early long-cycle calendars measured the angular displacement among the apparent movements of the dots, not what empiricists, such as Galileo, have crudely, and wrongly presumed to be a factor of pairwise distance between the intervals of observed movement of the dots themselves. The successive work of Kepler, Huyghens, Leibniz, Gauss, and Riemann, has confirmed that the system of Solar orbits is of the Kepler-Gauss, or so-called hypergeometric form of curvature.[23]

The re-creation of that experience of mankind during pre-historic and ancient historic times, ought to be an integral, and crucial part of the activity of the pupils, even at pre-secondary levels. Rather than at-

---

22. For a currently estimated two millions years, the Earth has been dominated by recurring "ice ages." These are chiefly periods of massive glaciation on the land masses of the northern hemisphere, alternating with shorter, interglacial warming intervals, during which the ice-freed land-areas of the northern hemisphere have been approximately those of the interval from 4000 B.C. to the present day. Thus, the level of the world's oceans prior to the current warmer phase, was about 400 feet lower than today. These ice-age cycles are, predominantly, associated with a long-wave periodicity within the Earth's solar orbit. The world is presently in a long-term cooling phase, headed in the direction of a new ice age. Only profound and sweeping changes in prevailing economic policies, toward forced-draft investment in fundamental scientific progress, could prevent the world from being plunged into a new ice age during the few thousands years ahead.

23. The terms "hypergeometry" and "multiply-connected manifolds," are used interchangeably in the so-called "non-Euclidean" geometries of Gauss and Riemann.

tempting to interpret the mere words used to describe astronomical patterns, as today's superstitious believers in the cult of astrology do, the students should share the experience of the individual pupil's direct observation of the night sky, as ancient man first adduced the idea of fixed universal laws from such observations. The idea of *validatable universal physical principles*, has been developed in known history, chiefly as a by-product of the development of empirical astrophysics, into the direction of the conceptions established by the successive development of astrophysics by, chiefly, Kepler and Gauss. Physics means, chiefly, the search for the same quality of validatable universal physical principles in the very small, as astrophysics defines universal principles empirically in the very large. The study of such principles operating at those extremes, is the standpoint of reference for the literate use of the term "universal laws" in all fields of inquiry.

There are four classes of observed effects, which taken together, form the evidentiary basis for all notions of objective, experimental scientific inquiry. These four classes of effects, and their adducible correlations, provide the foundations for all competent policies of science education in secondary and higher education today.

One of these, is experienced, as I have just emphasized, on the scale of astrophysics. A second, is experienced on the scale of microphysics. A third, is the clinical evidence of a qualitative, categorical difference, between living and non-living processes, even when the contrast is between observed processes composed of what are ostensibly virtually the same chemical materials. The fourth, is the difference between the mind of the human individual and the behavior of the beasts. The issue of the way in which living processes serve as the medium in which the development of cognition has occurred, is the key challenge for all the fundamental issues of modern scientific knowledge.

The definition of modern science, should be restricted to the study of the validatable discovery of those principles, which are equally valid in each of all four of these domains of observation. Principles which meet that qualification, are justly defined as validated universal principles of science and Classical artistic composition.

However, there is something more. The study of the history of man's increase, and failures to increase our power in and over the universe, per capita and per square kilometer of the Earth's surface, must be conducted in the light of those universal principles of science and Classical artistic composition. That study constitutes the foundation for a rational study of the principles of history. When we define the nature of the human individual's cognitive processes from the standpoint of such a science of history, and only then, do we begin to develop scientific knowledge of the universal principles which define man in the universe: man defined in terms of our species' unique capacity to increase its power in and over the universe.

That latter study defines the basis for *the science of physical economy*, the field of my professional concerns and special competencies. The proper purpose of educational policy, is to contribute an indispensable part to the cultivation of that unique potential which is lodged within the individual newborn member of the human species. The measurement of the performance of educational policies, is to be addressed from that standpoint of measurable performance.

5.2 The Mind of God

The crucial fact of history so defined, is that the unique ability of the human species, to increase man's power in and over the universe, is accomplished only in a combination of two ways.

First, there is man's discovery of validated new, universal physical principles. Without the application of these fruits of cognition produced as universal physical principles, man could not increase our species' power in and over the universe.

Second, there is man's discovery of universal principles of a Classical-artistic form, including the principle of national economy first introduced during Europe's Fifteenth-Century Renaissance. These principles provide man the power of cooperation, through which the discovery of new physical principles is promoted, and through which society defines those principles of cooperation upon which the adequate social application of universal physical principles, is accomplished.

Whenever mankind employs such discovery of universal principles, mankind increases our power in and over the universe. This is the fundamental principle of all scientific economics. No other species has this capability. This principle permeates all of Kepler's most important and absolutely revolutionary discoveries, upon which all effective modern astrophysics, and other modern physics is based. Repeatedly, as in his *The New Astronomy*, Kepler refers to the principle of *Mind* as the fundamental principle of astrophysics.[24] At this point, I am not presuming to describe the Mind of the Creator of our universe, but simply showing the implications of Kepler's use of "Mind," as in referring to "the Mind of the Sun," or that "Mind" of the planet expressed by its orbital characteristics. Kepler's use of the concept of "Mind" in this way, coheres with the reality of all competent trends within modern scientific thought.

Whenever mankind self-governs its own behavior according to validated discovery of universal principles, mankind's power in and over the universe tends to increase, as this may be measured per capita, and per square kilometer of our Earth's surface. This principle is otherwise known as the Classical definition of *Reason*. This notion of Reason coheres with Kepler's use of the term "Mind," as in his *The New Astronomy*. This same notion of Reason corresponds to the best usage of "The Will of God," in Christian theology, for example. When mankind acts according to Reason, so defined, mankind's power in and over the universe, is increased.

This power of Reason is, of course, what I have described as *cognition*, as the principle of metaphor in Classical artistic composition, as knowing must be contrasted to mere learning, as I have done in earlier portions of this report.

The notion of Reason which I have just described, appears in a significant approximation in even pagan Greek Classical thought, as Plato, and followers of Plato such as Eratosthenes, best exemplify this. It appears as the notion of the universe as founded, not in fixed forms of matter, but, rather, in a permanent principle of change, as Plato and other writers attribute such a notion to Heraclitus. Plato states his argument for

Statue of Johannes Kepler in his birthplace, Weil der Stadt, Germany. "Repeatedly, as in his The New Astronomy, *Kepler refers to the principle of* Mind *as the fundamental principle of astrophysics."*

Heracleitus' principle, in the form of an ontological paradox, in his own *Parmenides*.[25]

This permanent principle of change, has nothing to do with the mystical charlatanry of G.W.F. Hegel. It is

---

24. For this purpose, I have relied principally on the relevant original works of Kepler and Gauss. My studies have been premised, initially, on the German translations by Max Caspar; I have, more recently, compared the Caspar texts, including the *Weltharmonik*, with the English Donahue translation. The reader of this report is referred immediately to Kepler's use of this concept of "Mind," in his *New Astronomy*, trans. by W.H. Donahue (Cambridge, U.K.: Cambridge University Press, 1992), pp. 122-129.

25. The foolish, but commonplace pedantry respecting the reading of Plato's terminology, is to be viewed as a product of the mind-deadening effects of substituting mere learning for knowledge. In that defective, but all too widespread habit of the pedantic mind, laborious glosses on the sundry uses of terms, are used as a substitute for scientific method. In other words, to understand a report of a scientific discovery of principle, the student, or scholar must reconstruct and relive the experiment as implicitly described. The ideas to be adduced from important works, such as the writings of Plato, are those conceptions which can be validated as discoveries of universal principle. Once one has discovered that one's own mind has thought, cognitively, in this matter, as Plato describes the case, and only then, does one know that one's understanding of Plato's argument is coherent with Plato's own. All contrary pedantic glosses can then be relegated to the arcana of a modern academic Dr. Faustus.

known to every competently educated secondary student, the one who has actually re-experienced many validatable original discoveries by minds from earlier generations. The cognitive power of both discovering a true ontological paradox, or true metaphor, and solving that paradox by means of a validatable discovery of universal principle, is the universal principle of change known to the human mind. This is the principle of axiomatically non-linear change referenced by Plato, and in Leibniz's notion of a *monadology*.

Thus, it is only in those cultivated qualities of cognitive action, by means of which validatable discoveries of universal principle are generated, as solutions to either ontological paradoxes of science, or true metaphor, that the activity of the individual human mind corresponds to the Mind of the universe, as Kepler employs the use of "Mind" in *The New Astronomy*.

Admittedly, once we have gone that far in comprehending the fundamental principles of empirical scientific work, we are lured into what must seem to many as a "religious" assumption. If the universe created a being, cognitive mankind, whose characteristic activity, cognition, has the power to command the universe in ways consistent with the design of this universe, one is lured into asking: Perhaps the universe has worked to produce that special being, mankind, to be the companion and servant of the Creator? For any scientific mind, that is a very tempting thought. It is also a useful thought, inasmuch as it locates the human individual's efficient existence within what the best theologians have regarded as "the simultaneity of eternity." This is, indeed, the moral standpoint of an effective general policy of secondary and higher education.

5.3 The Philosophy of Education

Once we have located that principle of change, so situated, in respect to the role of validatable universal physical and Classical artistic principles, the science of physical economy becomes the location in which the performance of educational policies is to be measured.

What is being measured is the correlation between the effect of increasing the number and application of new discoveries of those principles, to the resulting increase of man's power to exist within the universe, per capita and per square kilometer of the Earth's surface. Since the root of this beneficial result is cognition, as I have defined that here, the efficient content of educa-

tion, and its benefit for mankind, are defined accordingly. We do not measure education as learning; we measure it as the cultivation of the cognitive activity of the individual, in respect to both universal physical and Classical-artistic principles. We measure, thus, the relationship between the cultivation of that cognitive activity, and the development of man's power in the universe. We measure that relationship in physical terms, as a physical process of cooperation among the members of society.

This beneficial effect occurs to the degree that society wills that result to occur. This occurs to the degree that society is able to predetermine such a result over spans of successive generations. It does not occur as the result of an accumulation of local actions in the short term.

Thus, the development of society, as Solon's reform at Athens typifies this, and, more emphatically, as the development of the modern sovereign nation-state republic best typifies this, has been the key development in bringing about the greatest rates of improvement in man's power to exist, per capita and per square kilometer. That latter advantage occurs only as the society as a whole, its government, assumes the responsibility for promoting the development of the individual person and land-area to this intended effect.

Since this process must be measured in terms of the span of generations, the beneficial result tends to occur, to the degree that the combined progress of public development of infrastructure and private economic initiative, work as the notion of "indicative planning" as defined by the de Gaulle Fifth Republic illustrates the point, and as the American System of Hamilton, the Careys, et al. defined this principle. This is shown most dramatically, by examining the way in which the U.S.A., as prompted by President Abraham Lincoln, led the world in the development of the modern agro-industrial revolution, during the interval 1861-1876. The effect of the U.S.A.'s first centennial exhibition, in Philadelphia, in launching the modern agro-industrial development of Germany, Russia, and other European nations, and the role of the American, Benjamin Franklin, in personally directing the beginning of the mid-Eighteenth-Century agro-industrial revolution inside England, are crucial demonstrations of the principle sometimes called "indicative planning." The study of the doubling of the economy of France, under the leadership of France's King Louis XI, is also of crucial importance for those who wish to see this in an appropriate historical perspective.

Those historical cases help us to recognize the folly of defining education as the student's learning of that which will, principally, qualify the future adult for obtaining and holding employment. That folly is to be traced to such origins as the same Code of Diocletian whose legacy misshaped the history of feudal Europe. That folly is characteristic of the oligarchic, as opposed to the republican view of society and the human individual.

Naturally, for the adolescent and adult who lacks a place of gainful employment, securing and holding such employment may become for him a very painful want. That pain may mislead him into being willing virtually to sell his soul to gain such employment, or more suitable employment. Often, that person does just that. Often, entire communities do the same, out of related motives.

The result, unfortunately, necessarily tends to be an inhuman one. The delusion, that the purpose of education is to qualify persons to hold employment, even improved quality of gainful employment, is one of the principal sources of the moral corruption gripping the ruined economy and people of the U.S.A. today. The resulting trend is to define actual people as we define cattle, as individuals to be taken from their stalls, out to work, and slaughtered when their work-contribution is no longer desired. The spectacle of people arising daily to commute to their assigned stall, and home again to do chores, to sleep, and perhaps enjoy a short period of mere entertainments at the close of the waking day, is not far from the transformation of a population of human beings, into the kind of human cattle which oligarchical power has always preferred.

My own personal experience is relevant. In what I do, I am a "driven workaholic." Sixty to seventy hours a week at work, is customary for me. I am relatively very good at my work. Most of it is centered around cognitive activity. Most of my life, my income has been at or near the poverty level, often most decidedly so; this has been the case, because of my devotion to what I recognize as the importance of my work, and the implied obligations I have incurred to my fellows on this account.

My life has become, thus, like that of a professional soldier, a patriot who plies his craft not for the pay, but because that is his profession. On this account, I am perhaps among the happiest of all professionals in the world today, as Leibniz, for example, defined happiness, and as our Declaration of Independence copied Leibniz on this matter of policy. I would wish that others enjoy a similar kind of personal happiness, although I would insist that they should also be paid well enough to maintain what is considered a normal, more or less self-sufficient personal life.

The objective of education must be to produce the cultivated mind of a future happy professional. If that student is developed as a cultivated mind, as I have outlined that development's principled features here, that student will come to typify a population which can do anything for which its present level of cultural development has prepared it. On this account, there should be no cattle-herding of the students in public or higher education. There must be the development of the individual pupil's mind, up to the level corresponding to the present accumulation of both universal physical and Classical-artistic principles, and history. It must be a student who has, in large part, relived the enactment of the great discoveries of principle up to the present time. It must be the development of cultivated minds who embody the living experience of the development of the cognitive side of culture, up to that time.

Employment policies in our society must be attuned to the employment of persons whose minds and hands have been cultivated in that way. Employers should return to the practice of employing persons who will be able to adapt to the tasks represented, and to develop in a progressive way, to higher levels of productive and related capabilities. Admittedly, one size will not fit all, but one educational cloth will provide the garment of useful employment for each. Policies of employment must be thus adapted to coherence with republican, rather than oligarchical conceptions of the role and requirements of the employee and professional in society.

5.4 The Issue of Standard Testing

Few worse follies have been imposed upon education, than the presently increasing, morbid obsession with computer-scorable varieties of "standard tests." Any political figure who supports such foolish policies, either has not learned to think, or knows virtually nothing about education, or is displaying a kind of contemporary political opportunism, which is currently about as popular as it is disgusting.

The auditing of the educational achievement of both the student and the relevant educational institution, must be based upon the cognitive principle. The areas of inquiry for this purpose, are the validatable form of universal physical principles, universal Classical-artistic principles, and a principled knowledge of history. The mode of the audit must be prompting the student to re-enact such cognitive discoveries in terms of some relevant, paradoxical topic with which the student was likely not to have been familiar earlier. No other kind of test, has any durable merit, or reliability as a standard.

Specifically, any standard testing based on mere learning, can yield faked results, and under competitive conditions among institutions and teachers, is likely to do so. The degree of cheating by the institutions, in institutions' preparing students for competitive examinations in learning, will naturally tend to exceed, by a very large margin, all of the cheating done among the students themselves.

Ask yourself a relevant question. If you were proposing to test George W. Bush's qualifications for President of the U.S.A., what kind of an examination would you design, which George might actually be capable of passing?

Actually, most of today's schools have already flunked any possible competent forms of testing, precisely because of the incompetent way in which learning is being defined and conducted currently. The proposals for use of competitive testing will only make the results of education worse.

The essence of the quality of performance of a good teacher, is the ratio of cognitive development to mere learning, conducted in the classroom and related personal study by the student. Largely as a result of the so-called cultural paradigm-shift which struck the students in secondary and higher education during the 1964-1972 interval, the attrition of time has brought about a disastrous lowering of the quality of education in the classroom and educational systems as a whole. What is being taught today, is, relatively speaking, induced cognitive illiteracy, as preparation for advanced degrees in rabid irrationalism.

What is needed is the uprooting of "home remedies" and other "patent medicine" for education. The emphasis must be on cognition in the classroom and personal study. To this end, the emphasis must be on a combination of the kinds of remedies which were likely to be accepted, still, among the best teachers in the best schools from the 1960s. Typical are reduction in class size, increase of the ratio of preparation to classroom work of teachers, increased pedagogical-laboratory and related programs, shift to emphasis on cognitively oriented Classical education, and the enrichment of schools with a newly developed elite of what might be called "beacon teachers." Federal assistance to public education should focus upon these improvements.

The latter will be teachers, qualified and increasingly self-skilled in cognitive approaches to education of pupils. Such a program of "beacon teachers," should be modelled upon the design of the original, pre-Napoleonic Ecole Polytechnique of Monge and Legendre, and also the Humboldt program of Classical Humanist education for Germany. The pilot reform introduced to Philadelphia secondary education by Alexander Dallas Bache, is also a model of reference.

Individual schools should be seeded with numbers of persons selected and trained to function as "beacon teachers." The emphasis in the selection, training, and assignment of these teachers, will be on Classical education and pedagogical-experimental programs. The standard lesson-planning and testing used in training and deploying "beacon teachers," will be the cognitive approach to education and auditing of students, with strong emphasis on pedagogical-laboratory approaches to providing the students familiarity with the notion of experimental validation of hypothetical principles.

Bringing back U.S. public education to the levels of competence commonplace during the 1960s, is a mammoth work. Retraining most teachers for that, will not be feasible during the short term. The feasible approach is to infect public education with cognitive influences, and let the success of cognitive methods spread the infection.

The fact that the existing, recent decades' trends in policy of practice have produced such a terrible result in so many aspects of national life, brings us to the kind of crisis-point referenced by Percy Shelley in his "Defence of Poetry." This is a time of crisis, when the population is ripe for a great increase of "the power of imparting and receiving profound and impassioned conceptions respecting man and nature." The institutions, and the general population are now ripe for sudden and profound reforms. Government must foster the emergence of the kinds of leadership needed within the pores of relevant public institutions.